bravo your life !

bravo your life !
mi soon burzlaff

Koryo Press
St. Paul, Minnesota

Bravo Your Life!

Koryo Press
St. Paul, Minnesota

www.koryopress.com

©2010 Mi Soon Burzlaff
All rights reserved. No part of this book may be reproduced, scanned, or distributed in any printed or electronic form without permission. Please do not participate in or encourage piracy of copyrighted materials in violation of the authors' rights.

Interior design and typesetting: Stephanie Billecke
Cover design: Ann Delgehausen, Trio Bookworks
Cover photo © Joanne H. Kim

Cataloging-in-Publication data is on file at
the Library of Congress, http://catalog.loc.gov.

ISBN-10: 1-59743-202-4
ISBN-13: 978-1-59743-202-3

Printed in Canada
15 14 13 12 11 10   1 2 3 4 5

This book is printed on acid-free paper.

"Mr. Kim," "Black Taxi," "Scooter Lesbians," "Happy Birthday," and "Yogurt" originally published in Korean Quarterly (Summer 2006: St. Paul, Minnesota). "Beauty and the Face," "Double Eyelids," "Moon," and "Pimple" originally published in Korean Quarterly (Winter 2006–2007: St. Paul, Minnesota). "Kimch'i" originally published in Heren (June 2007: Seoul, Korea).

bravo your life!

To all Koreans who study English, science, and math professionally from childhood, work long hours—day after day—with very little vacation, sing at the *norae bang* into the wee hours of the night, play computer games or surf the Internet incessantly, ride out-of-control buses every day, eat *ttŏkbokki* on the streets at midnight, work physically demanding jobs with very little financial or emotional compensation, live at home because you are well into your thirties and no one will marry you, dream of studying abroad for a better future for you and your family—all in the pursuit of making Korea what it is becoming: bravo your life!

아가씨	agassi	Unmarried younger woman, usually in her twenties.
아, 야	-ah	Suffix attached to the end of someone's first name as a term of endearment.
아저씨	ajŏssi	Man, mister, sir—title for men over thirty.
아줌마	ajumma	Married Korean woman, auntie, or ma'am—a word loaded with both positive and negative connotations depending on how it is used and the tone of one's voice.
아니요	aniyo	No.
안주	anju	Appetizers to go with alcoholic drinks. Koreans "need" anju when drinking wine, beer, or spirits.
아빠	appa	Father.
반찬	banch'an	Side dishes that are served with all Korean meals.
빨리빨리	bballi bballi	Hurry, fast, quickly.
비빔밥	bibimbap	Common dish of rice, various vegetables, sometimes meat, and a sunny-side-up egg. *Bibim* means to stir and *bap* means rice.
복날	bongnal	Specific day on the lunar calendar when the weather is very hot or very cold. Many people have chicken soup or dog meat stew on this day.
불고기	bulgogi	Thinly sliced, marinated, cooked beef.
작은언니	chagŭn ŏnni	Smaller sister—the second oldest sister in a family.
잡채	chapch'ae	Sweet potato noodles, carrots, spinach, onions, and meat mixed with sesame oil, sugar, and soy sauce.
청국장	ch'ŏnggukchang	Korean stew made from fermented soybeans—stinky, delicious, and healthy.
돌솥 비빔밥	dolsot bibimbap	Same as bibimbap, but served in a heavy, hot stone bowl, which gives the dish a crispy texture. The egg is uncooked because the hot stone cooks the egg as it is stirred.
학원	hagwŏn	Academies where most children study all subjects after school.
할아버지	halabŏji	Grandfather.

bravo your life!

할머니	halmŏni	Grandmother.
호박	hobak	Pumpkin—slang for an ugly woman.
인사	insa	To bow and pay respect.
가	ka!	Go!
개인택시	kaein t'aeksi	Taxi driver who owns his own taxi; the most common kind of taxi in Seoul.
갈비	kalbi	Grilled or steamed beef short ribs.
칼국수	k'alguksu	Knife-cut noodle soup.
감사합니다	kamsa hamnida	Thank you.
김밥	kimbap	Korean sushi roll filled with egg, spinach, radish, ham, and other veggies or meat.
김치	kimch'i	Spicy pickled or fermented mixture containing cabbage, onions, and sometimes fish, variously seasoned with garlic, red pepper flakes, and ginger. Served at every Korean meal.
건배	kŏnbae	Cheers.
큰언니	k'ŭn ŏnni	Bigger sister—the eldest sister in a family.
럭셔리	lŏksyŏri	Konglish term used by many companies to market products or a lifestyle. Often used to describe anything expensive.
맛있어요	masissŏyo	Delicious.
모기	mogi	Mosquito.
목욕탕	mogyok t'ang	Public bathhouse.
노래방	norae bang	Karaoke rooms, which came to Korea from Japan and are very popular.
오징어볶음	ojingŏ bokkŭm	Stir-fried spicy squid with onions and vegetables.
엄마	ŏmma	Mother.
어머	ŏmŏ!	Oh my god!
언니	ŏnni	Older sister—a title that a female gives a woman who is a bit older than she is, regardless if she is family.
오피스텔	op'isŭt'el	Konglish term for a building that is used for offices or studio apartments.
오빠	oppa	Older brother—many young women use this as an endearing term to describe their older male friends, boyfriends, or husbands.

vii

파전	p'ajŏn	Korean-style pancake made with vegetables and sometimes squid or seafood.
평	pyeong	A unit of measurement equal to about 35.6 square feet.
서비스	sŏbisŭ	Konglish for complimentary service. Given to customers everywhere, from grocery stores to gas stations.
소주	soju	Cheap, common, and strong Korean alcohol that costs around a dollar at local convenience stores.
탤런트	t'aellŏnt'u	Konglish word meaning actor or actress.
찜질방	tchimjil bang	Recent phenomenon in Korea where people wear matching t-shirts and shorts and relax in a co-ed, twenty-four-hour sauna/community setting. Restaurants, television, sports massage, Internet, and snacks are available.
된장	toenjang	Everyday soybean-paste stew, similar to ch'ŏnggukchang, but less pungent.
동네	tongne	Small town, village, or neighborhood area.
도와주세요	towa chuseyo!	Help me!
떡볶이	ttŏkbokki	Glutinous rice cakes cooked in a spicy red-pepper sauce. Sold at street stands and in restaurants.
우리	uri	Our—commonly used in place of the possessive "my."
원	wŏn	Korean currency: 1,000 wŏn is roughly $1.

church

We are in a sixth-floor church, which seems more like a converted warehouse room than the kind of churches I'm used to. It is cool from air conditioning, and I'm exhausted because last night I arrived in Korea for the first time since I was given up for adoption in the late seventies. As I desperately try to keep my eyes open, my mind is cloudy from the news that I will meet my birth family after the church service. Mrs. Lee, the mother of a Korean friend of mine in Minneapolis, found them.

The service is over, and a man in a suit leads me out first. Mrs. Lee and I walk toward the elevator, and instead of leaving, the man continues to guide us down a hallway toward a light. In seconds I hear loud crying, and women rush toward me calling my name, "Mi Soon-*ah!* Mi Soon-*ah!* Mi Soon-*ah!*" This happens so quickly that I cannot feel my body anymore. The women grab my arms tightly and lead me into a brightly lit room. There, on the sofa, are my parents with their heads down, looking at me, sobbing quietly. They speak in rapid Korean, words that I do not know, and I hear my name intertwined in their language.

The three other women are my sisters, and they touch my hands, arms, and thighs as I sit on the dry, brown leather sofa. They want me to repeat after them, *"Ŏmma! Appa! Ŏnni!"*

I barely say it, and they all clap their hands. They smile, talking and crying at the same time, while my friend's mother says, "They are very sorry. They keep saying how sorry they are to you. They worry you are angry at them."

I ask her to translate, "Don't be sorry. I am not angry. I am okay. I have a nice life in America."

The rest of Mrs. Lee's entourage takes pictures, as if this family reunion is a tourist attraction. They keep saying to me, "How do you feel? You must be so happy. Why aren't you crying?"

The light is bright and harsh. My face is blush and feverish; my hands are clammy as I stare at the red, puffy faces of my new family. I feel embarrassed. They look poor to me, and I pinch myself for thinking such a shallow thought. Tears keep pouring out of them, and for a reason I cannot explain, my eyes are dry: I can't even produce one drop.

makeup

The first things I learn when I meet my fourth sister are that her name, Minam, literally means *beautiful man* and that she recently married a kind Samsung salary man, Oh Sewon. It is only my seventh day with my birth family, and I'm staying at Minam's small but new apartment, located close to the Han River.[1] My three oldest sisters and mother are in the kitchen making *kimbap* and boiling eggs for our picnic this evening down by the river. Minam, my nieces and nephews, and I sit on the floor of her bedroom, and we look at her wedding albums.

    I get the feeling that my nieces and nephews have seen these photos many times. Minam has gained quite a bit of post-wedding weight, for she was super-slim in her photos. There are tons of pictures of her posing with her husband, almost like an American prom couple; she is in at least three different wedding dresses and one debutante-looking gown. Her hair is high up in a dramatic style, and her makeup is caked on heavily. She looks at each picture dreamily—in a way that seems like she is admiring a famous supermodel.

As we flip through the thick pages, she says at least four times, in English, "Am I beauty? Are you envy?"

I feel a little uncomfortable with her odd questions, so I finally say, "Yes, you are beauty. I am envy."

She pats my hand, "Mi Soon-ah, don't worry. You will have wedding, too." We reach the last page of the first album, and it's a picture with the families of Minam and Sewon. I recognize my parents right away—my mother wears her signature fuchsia lipstick and her French-roll hair attachment, but my father looks a little different. Minam says, "Is father funny? He wears my powder makeup."

I give her a strange look. "Why?"

"I say to father, 'Please-please wear makeup because I don't want red *soju* drinking face in wedding picture.' I beg and beg him and he says 'okay,' and I put many-many makeup on him." She laughs nervously, and I do as well, because I'm beginning to realize how much soju my father really drinks.

All I can think to say is, "You did a really good job with his makeup."

Admiring the picture a little more, she smiles with pride. "Thank you. I will do his makeup for your wedding, too."

miok

We are in the cheerful and overly decorated living room of Miok's small Daegu[2] apartment. She is my third sister. I speak no Korean; Minam speaks a little English. Miok speaks no English, yet she has so much she needs to say to me. I sit on the light-yellow leather sofa. Minam sits next to me; Miok sits on the floor in front of me. She holds my hand and speaks Korean with a melancholy tone. Minam does her best to translate. Jagged sentences come out at a slow pace.

Miok is sorry.
Miok loves you much.
Miok is so sad.
Miok think your life sad because we gave you America.
Miok want care for you.
Miok happy you come Daegu.

Now they are both sobbing, almost uncontrollably. Time with my new Korean family is quite intense. Miok sees that I'm tired, so she takes my hand and leads me to my bed to tuck me in, holding and massaging my hands and arms as I fall asleep.

The next morning, the three of us arrive at Daegu Train Station. Miok secures a pass so she can escort us directly to the train, and as we wait for it to arrive, Miok won't let me go. She is shorter than me, but she stands behind me, hugging me tightly as if I might fall apart. The train slowly approaches, and we watch the carriage numbers perfectly line up with the platform numbers. Miok reluctantly releases me.

After we settle into our seats, I look out the window; Miok looks at me sadly, waving, trying to hold back her tears. She was only twelve when my mother returned from the hospital without me, old enough to remember, yet too young to have to experience the loss of a baby sister. The train begins to move, and Miok begins to walk with it, keeping eye contact with me the whole time. It's like a scene from a film, but there is no romance or unrequited love in this picture. The train gains momentum, and Miok jogs a little, then runs. She can't keep up with the inevitable speed, although she tries her best, almost sprinting now. I turn my head away for a split second, trying to suppress my tears, and when I look back, she has become a speck and disappears.

kiss

Tonight, most of my family will sleep over at my mother and father's home. Since my second sister lives below them, everyone runs in and out of both apartments.

I can't fully explain why, but my father makes me uncomfortable. His constant state of soju haziness is something I'm not used to, but I'm well aware my Korean family deals with it every day. All the sisters can tell that I feel strange around him, and I almost feel like they have become my bodyguards when he is near. He talks so loudly. His face has a constant red hue, and his breath is strongly affected by his morning, afternoon, and evening soju fix.

He has been warned over and over that he needs to stop drinking—that he will die from liver failure—but everyone knows, including him, that it is impossible for him to quit drinking, let alone reduce the amount he drinks.

As my sisters run in and out—chopping vegetables, cooking, cleaning, running after *Chagŭn Ŏnni's* toddler son—a brief moment opens up with just my father and me.

We look alike, even though the booze and years of hardship have been unforgiving to his face. We have the same eye shape, eyebrows, and nose. He is proud of this.

I sit on a chair. He walks over to me with tears in his eyes. I don't understand anything he says, except, "Yang Mi Soon." He stands behind me, and I can feel his body heat, even though there is no physical contact. I can tell he's reaching for me. He places a callused hand on my neck, and he begins to stroke my hair. I freeze, but I allow him to continue. He runs his fingers through my long ponytail while speaking to me in Korean and crying. Now he tries to tilt my head up and to the right so that I will look at him. I try to fight it, just staring forward, but he moves my head a little more forcefully. He tilts it enough to the right, and then he brings his face to meet mine and kisses my cheek with his tear-coated lips. I feel strange, but then he lays a big slobbery kiss right on my lips, making a loud smacking sound. I cringe and close my eyes.

Chagŭn Ŏnni walks out of the bathroom and quickly pulls my father away from me, scolding him for not staying away. He returns to the corner of the room, like a child who knows he has done wrong but couldn't help himself. I stay sitting on the chair, with my back to him, and Chagŭn Ŏnni hugs me from behind in a protective way while she strokes my hair. I can feel the weight of his helpless stare, even through her warm embrace. I feel safe and guilty.

hamburger kimbap

Kimbap is a Japanese import that has taken on its own cultural identity in Korean cuisine. It is seaweed laver filled with rice, strips of egg, and different vegetables along with Spam or ham rolled into the mix. Kimbap is cheap and semi-healthy, and it's served in small restaurants all around the country.

In my neighborhood, there's a popular place that's famous for its quality kimbap and *ttŏkbokki*. After my first few visits, they got used to my American accent, and I learned how to ask for my kimbap without ham. I don't eat any kind of meat, although some Koreans don't consider Spam, ham, or hot dogs actual meat.

The restaurant is always crowded at lunchtime, and it recently moved to a larger place just a few doors down from where it was. Today is my first time eating in the new space, and it's crowded with the usual lunch rush. I sit by myself in the corner, just happy to look like everyone else and blend into the crowd, a luxury that was never afforded to me in Minnesota. Since the space is at least three times bigger now, there are a lot of new people working. A woman comes over to take my order, and I'm disappointed that she's new. I say, "Kimbap ju-sae-yo. Ham bbae-go."[3]

She looks at me impatiently and loudly says, "Hamburger eobsseoyo! Hamburger no!"[4] People are beginning to stare. My face is red.

I try to make my pronunciation better and say my order one more time. "Kimbap ju-sae-yo. Ham bbae-go."

She really is frustrated now. Koreans aren't used to anyone speaking their language as a foreign language, and she says even more loudly, "Hamburger eobsseoyo! No! Hamburger no! Hamburger eobsseoyo!"

The place is dead quiet now, and I want to sink under the table as everyone stares at the freak trying to order a hamburger in a Korean restaurant. Finally, one of the regular employees recognizes me and announces to everyone, "She doesn't eat meat. She doesn't eat ham!"

The lady chuckles a little and walks away. The restaurant returns to its normal frantic buzz as people shovel in their food as quickly as it was made and brought to them. My no-ham kimbap arrives shortly, and a few people give me curious looks; I shrink over it and eat it as fast as I can.

black taxi

I've never taken one of these taxis because I'm afraid of them. They are *lŏksyŏri* style, expensive and shiny black. The basic fare is at least twice as expensive as a regular taxi. Usually businessmen and people who don't care about the cost of things take these black taxis.

Since it is raining, and I've been waiting for over half an hour, and every taxi is full, I decide I will take any available taxi that comes along.

I don't have an umbrella, so I'm standing a little way back under the shelter of the stairwell roof. Even though I was here first, two twenty-something Myeongdong[5] princesses (with umbrellas) stand in front of me. Now the taxi will stop for them first. I feel a bit bothered by this, so I stand out in the acid rain, leaving my shopping bags sheltered. The two princesses flash me a mean look, laced with a bit of pity, which I think is because I'm soaked and still in my work clothes, while they stand there in their high heels, mini-skirts, and stylish accessories.

Taxis keep flying by with drenched passengers wearing relieved looks on their faces, and finally, a shiny black taxi with a red "empty car" light approaches. I don't care how expensive it is because I'm cold and soaked and want to go home. I feel entitled to this taxi. I know I was here first. As the taxi comes closer, I hear the princesses say, "It's the expensive one. We can't take it." I put out my hand, and the taxi stops right in front of me. I turn around, reaching for my bags, and as I'm about to open the door, the taller girl aggressively taps my shoulder and says, "Ŏnni, we were here first. So, we'll take this one." They flash smug grins and hop in.

I just stand there—wet, speechless, and defeated.

kimch'i

My American family is visiting Korea to see me and to meet my Korean family for the first and probably only time. I'm still torn by the *Sliding Doors* experience of it all, getting to know my Korean family, seeing what my whole life would have been like.

My Korean parents' humble, two-bedroom apartment is filled with a variety of people: my American parents, Julie and David; my older sister, Sulynn, adopted from Korea a year before me; Peg, Rob, and Becca, family friends of ours; and my entire Korean birth family. My American mother is a retired elementary schoolteacher. She is positive and pragmatic; she has always supported me. Sulynn never had any real interest in searching for her birth family, and she truly assimilated. Peg is a kind-hearted, selfless social worker who comes to Korea twice a year to place physically or mentally disabled Korean children in Minnesotan homes. Her daughter, Becca, was adopted from Korea, too. Becca truly wanted to meet her birth family, but there was no real information, except that she was abandoned by them when she was a very small child.

As my American "delegation" and my Korean family sit in this same space for just one afternoon of their lives, I have a hard time getting my head around it all. There are too many complicated thoughts and feelings that everyone seems to emit subconsciously. What a random mix of people in this tiny Seoul apartment. People like my Korean parents have very little furniture, so all of us sit on the semi-soft, clean floor except my American father, who has a bad back; he sits on the one chair they own.

The time goes by quickly. We eat *chapch'ae, p'ajŏn,* and *bulgogi,* all Korean dishes that aren't spicy. Fruit platters are served and presents are passed around. Ŏmma has had most of her 18 kt gold jewelry melted into a necklace for Mom, and in return, Mom gives her a beautiful hand-stitched quilt she made with my dear Grandma Boettger. I translate as best as I can, but I feel stressed—just too much pressure—and I act immature and cold.

Peg says, "Mi Soon, I noticed there was no *kimch'i* on the table. Does your mother make her own kimch'i?"

"Yes, she makes her own, but I think she didn't put it out because she thought it would be too spicy for all of you." I translate this to Korean, and Ŏmma nods her head at my correct assessment.

Peg says, "Oh, that's too bad. We would like to have tried her kimch'i." I translate this, too, and Ŏmma's eyes light up. Koreans are proud of kimch'i, especially the ones who make their own. Even though my Korean family is working class, they own a kimch'i refrigerator, as do all of my married sisters, since it preserves this daily food at the ideal temperature. Kimch'i is as important to Korean culture and cuisine as bread was to American culture before Dr. Atkins. Although the two floor tables have been cleared and we sit around munching fruit from the platters, Ŏmma runs to her kimch'i refrigerator and begins to make a small sample plate. I begin to freak out, imagining our visitors with their mouths on fire, asking for more and more water, which will only add flame to their burning mouths. I try to nix the kimch'i taste test.

Mom pipes in, "Oh no. I would love to try her kimch'i." She is trying to be a great sport, but I know the only spice that has ever touched her mouth is Mrs. Dash; she doesn't even like garlic. I try to translate to Ŏmma that my American family never eats spicy food, but she already has the sample plate ready. I'm touched that she is so proud of her kimch'i and that Mom is eager to try it. Ŏmma brings over three kinds: radish, radish greens, and the most common one—cabbage. She also carries over a small bowl of water. As Mom and Peg try to sit as comfortably as they can on the floor, Ŏmma takes the kitchen scissors and cuts each kind of kimch'i into small pieces, dips them in water to rinse off the red pepper flakes, and holds out the various kinds for them to sample. I feel unstable at this point, and as I try to translate everything, I become rude.

I say to Mom, "It's going to be really spicy. You don't have to eat it."

With a schoolteacher smile, she replies, "Of course I want to try it. I came all the way to Korea to eat kimch'i!"

All eyes are on Mom and Peg as they take the kimch'i from Ŏmma's hand and pop it into their mouths. They smile and make nice comments about it. Mom doesn't even ask for water; I'm proud of her. Ŏmma is beaming. She offers a small piece to my American father, and he declines, saying it's way too spicy; I'm disappointed. How can I begin to explain, describe, or even understand what it must feel like for my two mothers to meet under these circumstances? They are not threatened by each other; they love and appreciate each other, even though they cannot say two words of the other's language.

Often, middle- to upper-middle-class Western white people adopt non-white children from developing countries; wealthy white people adopt white children from their own country—unless you're Angelina and Brad. Adoption is not equal. It will never be until the day middle-class Asian or African families adopt white children from the States or Western Europe. As long as adoption exists on an unequal playing field, I hope the mothers and families involved have the same heart, maturity, and strength that both of my mothers possess.

My mothers' time together is almost over; they will never meet again, but they will always ask me about each other. My American mother never ate kimch'i before, and she will probably never eat it again, but she ate it today because she loves me—because it is her way to appreciate and respect my Korean mother.

mr. kim

For the past year, I have been teaching English classes for children and adults. Mr. Kim is often the only student to show up for my class. A high-ranking salary man at the Bank of Korea, he is quick to tell me that he punches in among the top 5 percent of earners in the country. He's in his late forties, loves to take long walks to work, and is an ardent Buddhist, with the exception of late drinking nights with his friends and colleagues. He loves to talk about young, beautiful girls, and he's been married for over twenty years.

I bring an article to class about a recent "groundbreaking" Korean drama series. It was about a young woman, plump by Korean standards, on the verge of *ajumma* status. She was a baker who had fallen in love with the handsome, wealthy owner of the bakery. In Seoul, thin is *in,* along with any procedure to make a young woman more beautiful, because owning beauty often means financial security through marriage. But in this series, the protagonist didn't have a size-2 waist, and yet the prince was still interested in her.

The article discussed a recent study in which Korean women were ranked in beauty from 1 to 5, with 5 being the most beautiful. It found that as the women's rank increased, so did their husbands' salaries.

I ask Mr. Kim what he thinks of this, and he fully agrees with the findings. In his unique accent and gregarious voice, he says, "And, the more power you are, the more beauty your secretary is."

"Really? Is your secretary beautiful?"

"Yes! Yes! Very, very beautiful! Miss Yang . . . do you think you are beautiful?"

I'm surprised by his question, although I'm pretty used to the subject of beauty in Korea, so it doesn't feel that strange. "I don't know. I'm just regular."

Mr. Kim definitively says, "Miss Yang. You are a 4."

"Oh, um, okay . . . I guess you just ranked me."

He nods his head up and down, then smiles. "Let's take a coffee break!"

dog meat

My class full of elementary schoolchildren is easily split between those who have tried dog meat and those who would never touch it. Although I strongly disagree with the way that some large Korean dogs are hung upside down and slowly beaten to death so the meat is more succulent, I don't often voice my opinion on dog meat dinners, because I'm not bothered if Koreans eat it: it's their culture.

Today, almost in a daring way, the children bring up the subject of dog meat stew during our class lesson about food. They are well aware of the attention Korean dog meat gets from the international media. I say to them, "Do you like dog meat?" Some students proudly nod their heads up and down, while others make childish squeals and shake their heads back and forth. "Okay, raise your hands if you don't like dog meat." At least half of the children raise their hands and smile at each other.

A charming little girl who takes the English name Lily says, "I don't eat the dog! I have the dog at my house!"

I say, "No problem, but who likes to eat dog meat?" An outgoing girl, Lisa, shoots her hand up into the air with pride and conviction, along with a very sensitive boy, Jay. Others in the class raise their hands slowly, trying to avoid eye contact with the students who don't eat dog meat.

With her hand still in the air, Lisa takes over. "Teacher, I like snake too! Who eats snake?" All of the hands come down, except for Jay's. She continues with a competitive tone in her voice, "Do you eat frog?" His hand stays in the air proudly. She goes on. "Do you eat horse?"

He says, "Yes, I eat it once." All the other children are amused as they quietly watch the meat showdown between Lisa and Jay.

Finally, she says, "Do you eat skunk?" The other children all make sounds of disgust. Jay shakes his head and slowly puts his hand down, disappointed in his defeat.

He accusatorially asks, "Where did you eat the skunk?"

"In the mountain—one time."

I'm a little surprised myself. "Did you like it?"

She simply shrugs her shoulders. "Yeah, it's okay."

The other children stare at Lisa in awe and quietly whisper, "Wow." Lisa finally puts her hand down: she wears a victorious smile.

shoebox

When my boyfriend Peter and I lived in the States, we had a beautiful, spacious apartment on Lake Calhoun in Minneapolis. We shopped at our local co-op every weekend, buying the most reasonably priced organic produce and other goods. We rode our bikes everywhere. We were happy and had a nice life together.

Now he lives in Seoul with me in my one-room flat, which is only a little bigger than our old bathroom, and we have six months to go before my lease is finished. Having no space is quite a change for us, and some of the time it is okay, but lately it isn't. Many nights he takes his students' papers into the bathroom for some late-night grading, and because of my early schedule, I run the blender at high speed at seven in the morning, making my morning smoothie. Adjusting to our conflicting time schedules and absolute lack of personal space means frequent fights, revealing much more in one month than we knew about each other in our first four years together.

Sometimes when he gets really frustrated with me late at night, he heads down the street to the closest fried chicken shop to grade papers or read a book. He doesn't eat meat, but it's as good a place to work as any in Bomun.[6]

It's a little past midnight, and it's my turn to storm dramatically out of our fourth-floor shoebox. Where do I go? I hate chicken, and the buses and subway aren't running anymore. I brusquely grab my cell phone and iPod, step onto the ocean of shoes gathered at our front door, and shove my feet into any pair that fit. Opening the door I say, "I'm going out. Don't wait up for me!"

"Fine with me. I'm going to sleep now."

It's not quite spring, but it feels warm enough, so I just walk around the streets for a few minutes. I have no idea where to go because I left in such a huff that I have no money with me. Our *op'isŭt'el* has eight floors, and adjacent to the building is a large set of stairs that lead up a big hill to a small alley, right at the fourth-floor level of our shoebox. I find it comforting to know that if a fire broke out, I'd have a semi-easy escape; but if I missed the four-story pillar wall, I'd have an awful fall. There are two short concrete pillars at the top of the stairs, so I plop myself down on one and turn on my iPod. With my arms folded, listening to Marvin Gaye, thinking about how much I hate my life and Peter right now, I realize how freaking cold it is. I am literally sitting right next to our shoebox. I see Peter's silhouette laying the Korean mattresses down for our bed. He turns the light out.

Still fuming, I whip out my cell phone and call him. "Peter, this is me. Could you open the window and hand me a jacket?"

His tired voice says, "What? What are you talking about? Where are you, darling? Just come home."

"No, I'm cold, and I just want you to open the window and give me my jacket." He pauses for a few seconds, and I tell him again to open the window. He turns the light on, walks over to the window, opens it, and looks at me like I'm a psycho.

"Sweets! What are you doing there? Just come in and go to sleep!" I order him for the last time to give me my jacket, and he finally capitulates. As he tries to hand it over, it's too far for me to reach, so he uses a hanger to get it to me.

All I say is, "Thanks, Peter." I put on my jacket, and he flashes a confused look at me and closes the window. I return to my concrete stump, sit there for thirty more minutes, walk down the long set of stairs, take the elevator up to the fourth floor, and quietly walk back into our shoebox. Peter pretends to sleep.

bus 1111

A little boy timidly steps down from the bus stop curb. The door on the 1111 bus opens as it comes to an abrupt stop. He nervously asks, "*Ajŏssi*. Do you go to Han Sung University?"

The driver says, "*Bballi bballi!* Hurry, get in!" The boy can't be more than eight years old, and he clearly doesn't take the bus alone very often; he pauses a brief moment to process the information.

The bus driver yells more loudly at him while revving the engine, "Hurry up!"

The little boy nervously steps onto the bus, but the driver can't wait and begins to speed off the second the boy's foot makes contact with the first step. The boy loses his balance and almost falls back onto the street. With a ghostly look on his face, he grabs the door and rushes up to deposit his thousand-*wŏn* bill into the box. His eyes are as wide as a baby doe's in danger. He pockets his change and takes a seat as quickly as possible.

The bus driver rushes forward about thirty feet, only to slam on the breaks for the next traffic light. He was about to speed through the red light and crosswalk, but he had to stop for the pedestrians crossing the street. Young mothers, college students, and grandparents are riding this bus, and no one seems bothered by the danger this little boy was just in.

happy birthday

I am sitting in the basement of an Insadong[7] restaurant. It is lovely and modern, and it serves Jeonju[8] *bibimbap*, known for its many ingredients that give it a distinctive and more luxurious taste than regular bibimbap.

Sang-beom—or Franco, which is the English name he has chosen—sits next to me, and his aunt is taking us out for dinner. I've tutored Franco for over a year now, on and off, and just before dinner we translated his story "Learning to Ride a Bike" into English for his school's annual speech competition. I felt sadly proud of myself for understanding an eleven-year-old's short essay.

His aunt orders *dolsot* bibimbap, and shortly after, three piping-hot stone bowls filled with rice, vegetables, a freshly cracked egg, various nuts, ginseng, ginkgo, and jujubes, along with the signature spicy red pepper paste, are placed in front of us on our low table. The floor we sit on is heated, and to me this is a commonplace luxury that everyday people in other countries never get to experience.

bravo your life!

We begin to stir the ingredients because that's the first thing you must do to eat bibimbap. I notice there is a little meat in my bowl, so I begin to awkwardly remove the meat onto a small napkin in the least offensive way possible. His aunt sees me doing it, and says, in Korean, "Put the meat in Sang-beom's bowl. He loves meat."

Franco cheerfully says, in English, "Oh yes. I sure love meat." I begin the transfer from the napkin to his bowl and then from my bowl to his bowl. We are eating in silence, since Koreans don't usually talk when they eat. This used to make me feel uncomfortable, but now I find it comforting. They just chew, and it all happens very quickly, like most things in this society.

As I eat, I look around the restaurant, and there is a lovely family sitting by the window, on the floor, a few tables away from us. It's a family of fourteen with parents, children, aunts, uncles, and grandparents. I see a little girl open her flute case. She quietly, and very shyly, puts her flute together. Her mother says, "Stand up. Don't be embarrassed," as she takes out a round birthday cake. It's the grandmother's birthday, and the mother lights the candles on the cake as the little girl begins to cautiously play the happy birthday song. Her whole family supportively sings along, matching their pace with the slow pace of her playing.

The song is finished. The family claps, and the little girl flashes a nervous smile, sits down, and quickly puts her flute back in its case. Franco and his aunt didn't seem to notice the precarious birthday tune coming from the flute, nor did anyone around us. Maybe they don't care. Maybe the restaurant is too loud. Maybe it's because this song is one we've all heard and have sung too many times. Though I blend in with all Korean faces, I often experience this culture as an undercover foreigner, and I feel touched by this scene.

1,000 wŏn

I sit on a bench opposite the front door, which faces Bomun subway station, while the shoe doctor examines the five pairs of shoes I just brought in. They are either new and need protective soles on the bottom or are old and need some kind of repair. In the States, I would have thrown away perfectly good shoes that only needed new soles, but in Korea, shoe hospitals (which is the literal translation) are abundant and relatively inexpensive. This shoe doctor is one of the best, as I am told by the middle-aged ajumma who hangs around at the front door, chomping her gum loudly and talking to the customers and the shoe doctor in an almost flirtatious way.

    She picks up my shoes and comments on how pretty they are and what good Italian quality they have. I thank her and wait patiently for him to determine if he has the necessary materials, how much the job will cost, and when it will be finished. Most shoe hospitals are metal "boxes" on the streets, which you must duck into or you'll hit your head, but this one is fancier—it's actually a shop that is part of a building on the main street in Bomun.

As the shoe doctor looks at the fifth pair of shoes, a homeless and, most likely, mentally impaired ajŏssi walks in the door. He wears old clothes, and his face is sweaty, tired, and covered with dirt and grease. He stands quietly at the door, not saying a word, but with his right palm out.

The shoe doctor looks up at him blankly and says, "No. I don't have anything for you," while the ajumma continues to snap her gum, trying to ignore him. The homeless ajŏssi won't budge, and he remains standing there with his right hand extended even further.

I open my wallet and quickly hand him a thousand-wŏn note. The homeless ajŏssi thanks me and leaves, while the shoe doctor gives me a puzzled and disappointed look. "Why did you give him that? Do you know what he will do with that?"

Even though the shoe doctor and I are friendly, I'm annoyed and say, "If I have money, I should help people like him. He needs it."

"But all he's going to do with that one thousand wŏn is buy soju. He needs to work. He walks around all day and gets money."

My Korean begins to fail me, but I try my best. "Even if he gets money during the day, I don't think he lives a nice and comfortable life. I think his mind is sick, and he needs help."

The ajumma jumps in. "It's her choice. She can do what she wants. She has the money. Look at her expensive shoes."

bravo your life!

The shoe doctor reluctantly puts down my fifth pair of shoes and says, "The total is thirty-eight thousand wŏn, and they'll be ready by next Monday."

At these kinds of places I must pay in cash. I open my messy wallet, noticing that it's full of a mixture of denominations and receipts, and take out whatever is in there, worried I'm a little low on money. I begin to sort through it all, counting it, while the shoe doctor and the ajumma watch closely. As I count, they count silently but with their lips moving, and we finally say together, "thirty-seven thousand wŏn."

100-wŏn coffee

I don't see my second sister, Chagŭn Ŏnni, as often as I should. She's only one year younger than my eldest sister, and even though she was able to graduate from high school, unlike our first sister, who couldn't even enter middle school, Chagŭn Ŏnni currently has the hardest life. She is the mother of three growing and active boys, with her youngest just starting kindergarten and her oldest already in high school. Her husband is currently unemployed, so her meager salary earned from her labor as a cook must sustain their family.

I have just spent a "traumatic" night with my mother, sisters, and Taehui, Chagŭn Ŏnni's youngest son, in my 8 *pyeong* shoebox. We all breathe a sigh of relief as we inhale the polluted fall air on the street that leads us toward Kodae,[9] my new place of employment. We choose the first Korean restaurant we walk by for a breakfast of bibimbap and *k'alguksu* before we embark on our tour of the campus. After we order our food, I notice how tiny Chagŭn Ŏnni

bravo your life!

is, weighing less than the coveted fifty kilos that many Korean women semi-starve themselves to attain. Sadly, this is due to her stress, chaotic life, and lack of enough time or money to eat well-balanced meals.

The food arrives, and I watch my sisters and mother interact in a loud and jumpy way, as if a manic cloud follows them around. This must be genetics, because I've been known to be quite hyper myself, especially at five-star hotel buffets. They eat fast and chew as loudly as they talk, and we finish this meal in what seems like record time, with all of them clanking their chopsticks and dipping their spoons in and out of each other's dishes.

Most Korean restaurants have a small coffee dispenser for their customers to use after they finish their meals, serving instant coffee in small Dixie cups. Often it is free, but this restaurant charges a hundred-wŏn coin, the equivalent of ten cents in America. We wait outside in the cool October morning while Miok and Minam buy our coffee. As we wait, a mother-son fight brews between Chagŭn Ŏnni and Taehui, because she thinks he is misbehaving and whining too much, even though he has just spent the last eighteen hours trapped in my shoebox with his four aunts, mother, grandmother, and no friends or toys. She yells at him loudly, and he shouts back like an ajŏssi, even though he is only six years old. My family can't speak at a reasonable decibel level during normal conversation, so when they are in heated moments like this, it's on display for anyone to hear or see.

Chagŭn Ŏnni is so frazzled that, losing all patience with Taehui, she whacks him on his bum. He starts to wail, and now my mother and *K'ŭn Ŏnni* join in the fight, taking Taehui's side; all four of them are yelling at each other. Minam and Miok emerge with the coffee, and while K'ŭn Ŏnni comforts the crying Taehui, she quickly brings them up to date on the drama, while Chagŭn Ŏnni stands off to the side, seething.

Minam brings a cup of coffee to her and tells her to drink it and relax. Chagŭn Ŏnni aggressively grabs the paper cup and throws it at the brick wall. Minam says, "Why did you do that? Do you have one hundred wŏn to throw away?"

Chagŭn Ŏnni crosses her arms and stares at the ground like a scolded child who has just been made to admit that she has done something wrong. She says, "No . . . I don't even have one hundred wŏn to waste."

bus 1147

Bus 1147 is out of control. The other night, as I waited for a different bus, this bus drove by me so quickly that I don't think it could have gone any faster. In the darkness you could see the inside of the bus brightly illuminated, and at the back there was one lone passenger bobbing up and down with each bump that the bus hurdled over.

It's early in the morning, and I'm tired. Even though I know I should take the ten-minute walk to campus, I can't bring myself to trudge uphill alongside the crowded and polluted street, so I wait at the bus stop for either the 1111 or 1147.

The 1147 bus arrives in its usual fashion, barely stopping for you as you put out your arm, and then taking off the second you step onto it. Today the bus is empty, and the bus driver gives me the meanest look while I use my cell phone to pay the bus fare. I run to the back, not bothering to sit down because I'll be getting off in a minute, but then the bus driver begins to yell at me for no reason in very loud and rude Korean: "Young lady! Why did you take this bus? You should've taken the 1111 bus! Why did you take this bus?"

I'm surprised, but I fight back. "What are you talking about? I can take this bus because your bus number is on the bus stop!"

He continues to yell at me as we pass the next bus stop, and I scream back even louder. Our faces are red and hot, like we are dusted with red pepper flakes, and we keep yelling the same things at each other.

I push the button for the next bus stop, holding on to the pole as tightly as I can, bracing for the bus to halt, and he slams on the breaks so aggressively that even his body jerks forward toward the steering wheel.

Because my Korean is limited, but I'm so angry, I scream one last thing as I get off the bus. "Ajŏssi! I hate you!"

I walk to the left, huffing and puffing, ready to stare him down if he dares look at me, when he abruptly opens the door and shouts, "Young lady! I hate you too!"

"bogoshipda" (i miss you)

It doesn't happen often, but our entire family is together: parents, four older sisters, our younger brother, who is on military leave, and me. We eat in our usual dramatic and fast-paced way—loud talking and fast chewing—while downing chilled Cass beer and little glasses of soju. Sadly, I only understand a small percentage of the conversation.

After K'ŭn Ŏnni and Chagŭn Ŏnni do the dishes, we head down to the local *norae bang*. The second we arrive, everyone transforms into his or her singing persona. Minam, the youngest of my sisters, is fluent in Japanese and graduated from a university in Tokyo, and she begins to punch in cheesy J-pop songs. She sings passionately while Wongeun, our baby brother, searches for his favorite Korean hip-hop music. K'ŭn Ŏnni and Chagŭn Ŏnni help my parents find their favorite old-school Korean tunes, like "My Heart Hurts." After some dramatic dance moves and ardent singing from all family members, the microphone, remote control, and songbook have touched everyone's hands.

The song "Bogoshipda" appears on the screen. Someone asks who put this song in, and I sheepishly raise my hand. My sisters squeal with excitement and pass the microphone to me as it begins. It is a slow pop song and was used for a popular Korean drama, so even my elderly parents are familiar with the tune and simple lyrics.

As the Korean appears, I timidly begin to sing the song. I have an awful voice, weak and out of tune, but I still continue. I concentrate on the screen and sing the best I can, sometimes with mistakes and other times with fluidity. K'ŭn Ŏnni is feeling the music, and she stands up to hug me from behind, singing the lyrics in a helpful way, encouraging me to sing it loudly. My other sisters begin to yell at her for not letting me sing the song on my own. I don't mind singing a solo or duet, but K'ŭn Ŏnni pouts for a few seconds, takes a seat, and continues to sing the lyrics quietly in the corner. Now, all eyes are on me. I can feel how pleased they are—that I can not only read Korean, but also sing a song to them, when I could barely say hello when we first met. I belt out the last bit of the song:

> *I'm crazy from the love I remember*
> *Memories make me want to search for you*
> *I cannot explain why I love you more*
> *I cannot close the door on you*
> *I could die because I miss you*
> *I will die if I lose you.*

itaewon

Itaewon could be one of the strangest neighborhoods not only in Korea, but maybe in Asia. It is packed full of American military men, foreign English teachers, migrant workers from South East Asia and Africa, prostitutes, gays, lesbians, and mixed-race couples.

I rarely frequent this area of town because of the obnoxious US soldiers and strange *hagwŏn* English teachers who seem to live on a boulevard of broken dreams. I do come here for authentic Thai, Moroccan, or Indian food, though.

It's a Friday night, and everyone is out in full weekend gear. It's late, around ten, and the dark atmosphere is lit up with garish store signs and club lights. I stand within a group of at least twenty people, all waiting to cross the busy intersection, and I listen to a mixture of different accents speaking both English and Korean.

To the right I see around eight American military men together. They are loud, and of course I understand everything they are saying as they talk about what kind of "Korean bitch" they're "going to fuck tonight."

I turn to look at them briefly, and one of them notices my stare; he is a short, beefy white man in his early twenties. He motions to his friends, pointing at me. "Let's check this bitch out over here. Let's check out this fucking ho." I tense up as they invade my space, and in a jocular stance, with his arms open toward me, the beefy man confidently says, "Hey, baby. What's going on tonight?"

I'm in a very public place, so I reply in a rude tone, "Nothing's going on. Don't talk to me."

His tall, burly friend jumps in. "Hey. Your English is good. Where'd ya learn?"

I inch away, closer to the edge of the curb. "What part of 'don't talk to me' do you not understand?"

"You don't have to get all stuck up, bitch!"

The rest of them start to call me other bad names. I try to ignore them and just stare forward, and the light finally turns green. I practically run across the street, and Peter is waiting for me, right on time. I wrap my arms around him dramatically.

beauty & the face

A small face is one of the most important prerequisites for a woman to be deemed beautiful in Korea; the eyes must be big, the body must be waif thin, and the face, especially the jaw, must be small. If one isn't born with these coveted features, then cosmetic surgery can change that, and many people in their twenties or thirties succumb to this remedy, both men and women. The fashion style among women is very demure and ladylike, often dubbed *gongju byeong*, literally meaning "princess disease," with most young women wearing skirts and dresses with tons of ruffles, sparkles, bows, and chiffon—and, of course, the omnipresent high heels to top off any outfit, even cargo pants or baggy jeans.

Eun Sook is a student of mine, and although she doesn't have the smallest body frame or face, there is something delicate and lovely about her beauty that I don't think she is aware of. Today we are doing impromptu speeches in our class of ten students, and since the weather is gorgeous, we pack up our bags and make our way to a perfect outdoor spot behind the building. The class is mostly women, with two men. It is diverse by Korean standards, with people having many different majors along with a good age range.

The students draw questions out of a small box, and Eun Sook's question is: *If you could change three things about yourself, what would they be?*

We are sitting on a large half-moon bench, facing a center island with an entire circle bench around it. Eun Sook is standing in front of the island, about four feet from where we are sitting. She seems oddly comfortable in her insecurity, and her nervous smile exudes a quiet confidence. She stands there in her semi-fitted jeans, cotton t-shirt, and high heels, deciding to concentrate on only one thing she'd like to change. She says, "If I could change one thing about myself, I'd like my body to look more feminine, because my body is big and strong, like a man's."

Our class lets out a big sigh, expressing frustration, sadness, and understanding of this subject. The birds are singing behind us, and she continues, "I've been told by many people that my body is not like a woman's and that I have a big face."

When she says this, I am reminded of what two other young women told me the other day: "My face size is my daily stress."

Eun Sook points to a pretty young woman in our class who embodies Korea's ideal of beauty. "My wish is her. She is perfect to me. She has a small face and this kind of body," she says, making an hourglass shape with her hands. "She can wear beautiful skirts. That is my dream and the style I want." At this point we want to cry for her, because we are touched by her honesty and disturbed by the unattainable dream that many Korean women have.

She pauses another moment, and as she's about to continue, a security guard on his motor scooter decides to take a leisurely spin around the island, right between Eun Sook and the rest of our class. I honestly don't think he can drive any slower, and we are so wrapped up in listening and supporting Eun Sook, it takes what seems like the longest couple of seconds for us to realize what he is doing. On top of this, I know him because I greet him every time I come and go from the building. He flashes a laid-back smile and waves at me while he continues on his way, leaving a cloud of scooter exhaust in our faces. We wear confused looks, feeling like our sacred moment and space have been violated by an ajŏssi on a scooter, but then we begin to laugh at the randomness of it all. I break the silence and, not knowing exactly how to respond, offer some clichéd advice about everyone's inner beauty.

With a nod of her head, Eun Sook sits back down and says, "Teacher, I have nothing more to say."

moon

Eunjin has been on my scooter once before, for thirty seconds, when I drove her from our International Studies Hall to the Korea University front gate to meet her dinner date. We recently signed up for swimming classes after work, and tonight is our first session. It's always strange the first time you see a friend from work naked in a locker room or sauna. Yesterday I said, "Eunjin-ah, I guess we are going to see each other naked tomorrow." She just laughed.

I see her in the morning and ask her if she trusts me enough to drive her to my home for a yogurt smoothie, then up to the pool and back to her bus stop. She says, "Ŏnni, of course! It was my true honor to ride your scooter the other day."

I say, "It will be my true honor to drive you again." The day goes by quickly, and before we know it, we are relaxing at my house for an hour before our swim class. It begins to rain; we convince ourselves to go since we already paid our money, and she has her swim bag ready.

It's raining even harder now, but we take my scooter because the hill to the swimming pool is extremely steep. Eunjin and I are both scared of acid rain, and even though I think the helmets are enough, she takes out her umbrella. Holding it over us with her right hand, she hugs and holds on to me with her left arm. I concentrate on driving carefully in the rain, but I have to pick up speed to make it up the hill. We're halfway there when Eunjin says, "Ŏnni, I think maybe you should slow down . . . just a little," and I turn around to see her barely holding on to her umbrella, which is now inside out and really high in the air.

We put our bags in our locker. As Eunjin timidly begins to undress, I suddenly whip off my cargo pants and unbutton my shirt. Eunjin screams, "That's not fair! That's not fair. You changed at your house!"

I quickly say, "Sorry! I didn't want to bring a bag with me. You'll see me naked after class." She says okay and puts her swimsuit on as discreetly as she can.

Our class is scary because our young female teacher yells at us for swimming too slowly and puts us in the remedial lane. After class, we shower and avoid making eye contact or talking, but we giggle at the same time. As we leave the building, we are bitter about our swim teacher, because all day we had dreamed about a handsome male teacher helping us with our backstroke.

The rain has stopped. We make our way down the hill on my scooter, with Eunjin hugging and holding on to me tightly; we feel happy. As we enter the university side gate, I say, "Eunjin-ah. Look. It's a full moon. It's so beautiful!"

Eunjin takes a deep breath, sighs, and says, "Yes. It is so big . . . like my face."

bus 144

Anytime I take a bus in Seoul, all I can think is, how do we ride these out-of-control buses every day? Fellow passengers look downright tired from their impossible work or study schedules, the kind of tired that is only exacerbated by riding one of these speed machines back and forth to school or from work. I like the 144 bus, as it goes north and south of the Han River, doesn't hit too much traffic, and usually isn't that crowded. But tonight as it nears midnight, I find myself squeezed tightly into the crowd of passengers, like we are perfectly packed in a kimbap roll.

Often when passengers enter a bus and pay the fare, both they and the bus driver ignore each other, but tonight is different, as this bus driver gives a sincere smile and welcomes each passenger individually onto his bus. Some people stare at him blankly, while others reply with a greeting. To my surprise, this bus isn't whipping us back and forth, and we don't have to hold on as tightly to keep from being thrown to the floor, which, embarrassingly,

bravo your life!

has happened to me before. In Korean buses, the drivers usually play whatever radio station they want, and it ranges from news, talk radio, pop songs or old-school Korean music. Tonight there is no music. Even though the bus is packed, the atmosphere is quiet, which is unusual, because a few people almost always talk loudly on their phones. After a bout of traffic, we hit a free stretch of road, and suddenly the bus driver's voice comes over the speaker system. I see him holding the mike, like the kind American truck drivers use to talk to each other, and he begins by saying, "Ladies and gentlemen. How are you tonight? I bet you all are tired. You look tired. Are you?" No one responds to his question. He tries again, "Ladies and gentlemen, are you tired? Let's hear a 'yes' if you're tired."

I'm quite amused by this affable bus driver, and so are a few others, so we respond with a quiet "yes." The driver isn't satisfied with our level of enthusiasm, so he asks the question one more time. Finally, half of the bus responds with a loud, "Yes! We're tired!"

He says, "I thought so. That's why I want you all to sit back and relax, and think of my bus as your taxi. I will try to get you home as quickly as I can."

Instead of using the recording, he uses the speaker system to announce each bus stop. He continues to talk to us the entire ride home, and many people are starting to feel annoyed with him, but others find him quite entertaining. He says goodbye to everyone who exits. The bus begins to thin out and more people are able to sit down.

My stop is coming up, and I push the orange button. For the first time in my three years in Seoul, the bus driver makes a complete stop, then opens the door, and finally waits for all of us to exit before he gently takes off—without rushing to reach the impending red light. I walk to the left, where the bus waits, and as the bus driver looks out the window, we make eye contact. We *insa* and give each other a friendly wave, and the light turns green. I see him grab the mike once again, and he safely takes the rest of his passengers home.

parisienne

In Bundang, a wealthy suburb of Seoul, there is a hair salon named Parisienne. I went there over a year ago when it just opened. At that time, bangs were in, as many Korean actresses were sporting that look, and my friend Joanne Kim and I decided to jump on the wagon. She told me that the owner of Parisienne always listens to her and her mother and only does what they want. When I first met him, he assessed that bangs would work with my face shape, but not Joanne's. He was gentle, humble, and precise. He cut them nicely for me, which looked okay for about a month, but I immediately knew it was weird when the summer humidity came and they looked like crimped pubic hair covering my forehead. My hair identity seemed to tailspin from that point on, leading to too many of Korea's infamous magic straight perms.

Now I just want my naturally frizzy hair back. It's currently stick-straight at the bottom and frizzy from the crown to my chin. My bangs have finally grown out to the length where the magic perm starts. I'm paranoid in Korean salons, because I feel like stylists use the language barrier as an excuse to do whatever they want, so Joanne and I go all the way to Bundang to meet the Parisienne hair master again.

The second we walk through the door, I know I should trust my gut instinct and walk right back out. The owner has changed the name of the salon to his name and hung a huge wall-size photograph of himself—posing on one knee, with his chin propped up on his hand like he's a movie star. He has his hair slicked back, and he's wearing poser sunglasses as he cuts a woman's hair.

All I want is for him to cut off six inches in a straight line, so there will only be about three inches of my magic perm left. I can't ask him to cut off all of the perm, because then I won't be able to wear it in a ponytail. He starts to get upset with my request and keeps saying over and over that it won't look good. I continue to say that I don't care, I just want to wear it back in a ponytail for a few more months until I can grow it out completely.

In the meantime, Joanne, who has even curlier hair than mine, decides to get another magic perm. I ask her to tell him what I want, because I feel like he doesn't understand my Korean, even though my instructions are very basic.

He finally says he will do what I want, even though he strongly disagrees. In the shortest minute, he takes a razor to the bottom of my hair and hacks it off so quickly that there is no way I can tell him to stop. It is so uneven and jagged that I am speechless. He says, "The way you wanted it would have made it look worse. This gives it more texture."

I stand up, grab my bag, and pay the fifteen thousand wŏn. Trying to suppress my tears, I look at Joanne and say, "I can't believe this happened. I'm late and gotta go to work. I'll call you later." She looks at me with sad and worried eyes.

For days I am upset, and I try to formulate and practice my complaint in Korean before I call the owner. The next time I see Joanne, she says, "He has changed quite a bit, that Mr. Parisienne. Don't feel bad. He really messed up my hair, too. He fried it, see? It's broken off here at the root by my forehead and temples."

"I hate him. We need to file a class-action lawsuit against him. Give me his phone number."

Joanne is not as vain as I am, and for some reason she defends Mr. Parisienne; she goes on and on about how her mother and brother still trust him and how he always gives her brother the full treatment whenever he goes in there. "I don't care if he loves your brother so much, I hate him, and look what he did to our hair. So give me his number."

She refuses. "Well, Mi Soon, that's life. It will grow and it doesn't look that bad." I pull my hair out of my ponytail, and she looks a little surprised at how uneven it really is. "Yeah . . . I guess he really changed. That wall-size picture is new. It wasn't there last week."

escalator

Although Peter and I are an interracial couple, we do not represent the usual one in Seoul. Too many Koreans assume that when there is a white man and a Korean woman together, the man is American and the woman is a fallen Korean woman who can't get a Korean boyfriend. I, too, find myself staring at some obviously stereotypical, mixed couples with hypocritical eyes, especially the ones where the men are much older and heavier than their thin and attractive Korean girlfriends.

At times I am faced with my own guilt for having a white boyfriend; Peter knows and understands this. The other night we had dinner at a posh restaurant in Cheongdamdong, Seoul's playground for wealthy socialites and surgically enhanced people. A middle-aged ajŏssi was sitting next to our table on the same side as Peter, so only I could see his critical glare. He looked at me like I was a stolen national treasure. He would stare at me and then glance at Peter with aggressive and disapproving eyes. I finally said in my perfect English, "Can I help you?" He quickly retreated, said nothing, and didn't stare at us again.

Today we are at Lotte Department Store in Myeong-dong, riding the long escalator up to the Duty Free shopping zone on the tenth floor. I am one step above Peter, and I have my arms wrapped around him, hugging him as we ride the escalator. Many young Korean couples display physical affection in public, like hugging and holding hands. Out of the corner of my eye, I see a well-dressed ajumma and her husband going down as we go up. She looks at me in utter disgust, with her jaw dropped as low as it can go. I finally feel fed up with this curiosity, this judgment of Peter and me. She doesn't know that he is from Dublin and that we met at our university in America—that I am a Korean American adoptee who grew up in a mostly white Minnesotan community. She has no idea about our long history together. She rolls her eyes at me, and even though she is eight or nine steps below, I find myself shouting, "What! What are you looking at? What?"

I don't think she was aware of how obvious her disgust was, as she is taken aback by my abrupt reprimand. Her face becomes red. I'm a little upset with myself for my public outburst. Both guilty, we turn around, continuing on our separate ways.

best taxi

Joanne Kim, John Lee, and I just had a fun and funny night drinking in a hip and hard-to-find Daehagno[10] basement bar. We drank too many Jack and Cokes, and we had a few hours of fun dancing with three random salary men who kept taking our pictures with their Samsung cell phones.

After we say goodbye to John Lee, we have the choice between a Best Taxi service or a regular *kaein t'aeksi*. I say, "We gotta get that Best Taxi driver. It means he hasn't had an accident in a long time, like ten years I think." We run over and hop in.

Our Best Taxi driver gives us an eager smile; he has dark hair, shiny skin, and he's wearing a pair of big, semi-scary, yellow-tinted glasses. Immediately he notices our funny Korean, and—as he takes a dramatic right turn—we notice his bad driving. Joanne slides into me, and she asks, "Is he really a Best Taxi driver?"

I've lived in this city for over three years now, and for some reason I always think the taxi drivers try to take me the long route home. In my broken Korean, I argue with our Best Taxi driver. "Sir, why are you taking us this way?" He tells me his route, and I say, "No—no—no, you should go that way." We argue a little more, and we're clearly annoyed with each other. Joanne just smiles and laughs, because we are a bit tipsy and keep sliding dramatically from side to side as he continues to drive like he's rushing us to the emergency room. The more we nervously laugh, the more he tries to show off, and his driving becomes even crazier. Finally we say, "Ajŏssi, are you really the Best Taxi driver?"

"Yes, I'm the best, and the route you want to take is bad. You should let me take you the way I know."

"Okay, okay. Go your way," and all three of us laugh uncontrollably for no apparent reason. He takes an abrupt U-turn, and Joanne whips out my digital camera.

"Let's take some pictures. Is that okay with you, sir?" In a matter of seconds, we squish our bodies way over to the left, behind his seat, and we start to pose with him every few seconds; he makes sure to tilt his head to the right and smile for each picture. The three of us act like childhood friends experiencing a digital camera for the first time, showing off each picture as we take them, except that he's fifty-something and our Best Taxi driver, and we are in our late twenties and don't know him.

He takes one last crazy left turn down my small alleyway, and we pose for our final picture with the car stopped. We say goodbye, jump out of our Best Taxi, and walk home, scrolling through the pictures we just took. As I open the black gate to my house, Joanne says, "We should've gotten his e-mail address to send him the pictures. Sorry, sir," she shrugs her shoulders. "Oh, life."

worst taxi

After an impulsive late-night Dongdaemun[11] shopping trip, I just need to get home. I'm tired as I stand at the bus stop, crossing my fingers for the last bus or for a taxi that will accept my destination, but I'm not alone—at least a hundred other people wait next to me. Taxis roll by slowly with open front windows, while tired shoppers shout out their *tongne*, hoping for the mercy of one of the drivers. An inebriated and vocal ajŏssi curses loudly because three taxis refuse him in a row. The next taxi that refuses him begins to drive away, and instead of retreating back to the bus stop area, he orders the taxi driver to take him home and hits the roof of the taxi with his hands. He proceeds to cling to the car, sticking his arms through the half-open window, with his knees scrunched up and his feet hanging a few inches from the ground.

This is one of the largest intersections in the city, with at least five lanes on each side, and there is always traffic. There is a red light now, and the ajŏssi and taxi driver are screaming at each other while the man continues to cling to the car door.

The light turns green, and the taxi driver begins to take off. He starts to roll up the electric window and picks up speed, but the ajŏssi still holds on as everyone watches helplessly. Soon the driver is going fast enough that the man can't hold on anymore, and his body drops to the ground; his legs are run over by the back tire. He is in agony and crying loudly in the middle of this crazy intersection. Three young men run after the driver, swearing at him, while the rest of the cars ignore this scene and drive around him. They return and try to lift him out of the middle of the street, but he's in too much pain and screams even louder. Many of us who are watching are upset and crying, and now a new batch of buses and cars approaches this part of the street. The young men make a barrier, telling the cars and buses to go around them, but the drivers impatiently honk their horns at the man, thinking he is just drunk and passed out in the middle of the street.

In the midst of all of this, my bus arrives. There is nothing I can do to help this man, so I get on the bus, still crying. The bus driver asks me what is wrong. I don't know the Korean word for car accident or how to say that a man was just run over by the worst taxi driver, so I put my left index finger in the air and say "ajŏssi," and then I use my right hand to say "taxi," and then I act out what just happened. I point to the man still on the ground and say, "He is really hurt." I take the seat I always take when I ride the bus, the one closest to the front door on the right, and I can see the bus driver's profile trying to process my strange hand motions and broken Korean. As he rounds the corner, right at the Dongdaemun landmark, he stops the bus in front of three police officers casually leaning on their car. He opens the bus door and tells them a man is injured about one hundred yards back.

He turns to me and says, "He will be okay." I thank him, but I don't think the man will be okay. I wipe my tears with my sleeve and sink down as low as I can in my seat, feeling so angry that this bballi bballi city is in such a dangerous hurry.

fart

Rarely does life introduce you to the kind of friend whom you love—like a true sister—from the first day you meet her. Joanne Kim and I feel so comfortable around each other that we sometimes shower together, watch TV in our underwear (if the weather is hot and humid), share clothes, talk about anything, and fart freely around each other. We can also fight and bicker like there is no day after tomorrow.

After we share *ch'ŏnggukchang* and *ojingŏ bokkŭm*, we walk to a bus stop and wait quietly. We feel full and satisfied. Because I don't eat meat or poultry, I eat loads of vegetables and fruit. I've always had a sensitive stomach; I'm embarrassed to admit this, but I can be gassy, especially if I indulge in a latte or French cheese. There is an ajŏssi waiting at the bus stop with us. I feel a fart coming on, and instead of holding it in, like I would if there were a handsome young man at the bus stop, I let it go freely; I'm surprised at how loud a sound it makes. Joanne and I cover our mouths in embarrassment and shock. We laugh out of discomfort, and the ajŏssi moves as far away as possible while still remaining at the bus stop.

Although she laughs, Joanne is a little irritated. "Why do you have to do that, man?"

"Sorry. I didn't know it was going to be so loud."

"Um. Yeah. That was really loud and sick!"

We begin to fight. "It's not healthy to hold farts in. It's just you and me—and him."

"That's what I mean. It's embarrassing. That man totally heard it and was grossed out."

"I'm not embarrassed. Why are you? It's natural." As our bus arrives, we continue to fight about the fart, but we become silent the moment we step on the bus. Ten minutes later we arrive in my neighborhood, and the second we exit the bus we begin to go at it again. Now we are becoming mean and intense—our night is on the verge of ruin. Joanne threatens to go home, and she crosses the street dramatically to catch the next bus. I follow her, yelling at her, and we stop in front of Paris Baguette, a bakery. She brings up the time I farted in a Thai taxi, and now we are screaming at each other at the top of our lungs—in English—absolutely out of control, to the point where people on the street gather to watch. We are immersed in our fight. There are some fleeting moments where we are on the verge of laughter, because it is ridiculous, but both of us have too much pride to give in.

An ajŏssi in a nearby car rolls down his window to take advantage of his ringside seat. Both Joanne and I give him a lethal stare and yell in unison, "Shut your window . . . Now!" He looks scared and immediately rolls it up. We both crack up, say "sorry," and hug. The crowd disperses. We link arms and cross the street.

"I'm sorry. I won't fart like that again."

"You can do it, kid—just when it's you and me."

fry pan: part 1

"I'm at your local supermarket. Is there anything you need?"

Ŏmma puts the phone down and screams at K'ŭn Ŏnni and Chagŭn Ŏnni, "Mi Soon's at LG Mart! Let's go!" She picks up the receiver again and says, "Wait a moment. We're coming down!"

Five minutes later, as I'm looking at bread and muffins, Ŏmma, K'ŭn Ŏnni and Chagŭn Ŏnni burst through the automatic door. They all talk at once, and I don't know who is saying what.

"Our pretty Mi Soon!"

"Have you been well?"

"Did you eat lunch?"

"Why don't you visit us more often?"

"Oh, you're so busy!"

"I miss you."

"I love you."

Ŏmma, ready to shop, takes off with a swift stride. She says in a commanding voice, "Let's go to the fruit!"

bravo your life!

We grab a cart and, with my approving smile, it fills to the brim with shampoo and conditioner sets, body soap, economy-size laundry detergent, and beautifully packaged boxes of summer Korean peaches. Ŏmma and K'ŭn Ŏnni are getting concerned about the price, and honestly speaking, I am, too, but my guilt from staying away so long has brought on this shopping trip. Despite our birth order, my two oldest sisters have had difficult lives, financially speaking, especially Chagŭn Ŏnni. She looks just as tired as the last time I saw her; her eyes are always dull and sad looking. I worry about her the most. She lives right above the poverty line.

Ŏmma runs off with K'ŭn Ŏnni to get come Coca-Cola, and Chagŭn Ŏnni and I roam the aisles. We stop at the section with cooking utensils, and we study the fry pans together. Chagŭn Ŏnni says, "Mi Soon-ah, can I get a small fry pan?"

"Of course! But don't buy that one. It's too cheap, and the quality is bad. Get this one."

"Oh my god! It's a Teflon. It's thirteen thousand wŏn! That's too expensive."

We argue a bit. As we finally put it into the cart, K'ŭn Ŏnni and Ŏmma return and immediately scold Chagŭn Ŏnni for selecting the expensive Teflon fry pan. They argue passionately, and I try to jump in to defend Chagŭn Ŏnni.

We finally make it to the checkout line. As they unload the cart, Ŏmma and K'ŭn Ŏnni are still complaining about the price of the fry pan. Chagŭn Ŏnni and I lock arms, listen to them, and nod our heads simultaneously, all the while smiling at each other.

fry pan: part 2

Miok and I wait—arm in arm—at the Daegu Train Station for Chagŭn Ŏnni and her youngest son, Taehui, to arrive. Miok and I are twelve years apart in age; we were both born in the year of the snake. She feels we have an extra-special bond because of this. I say, "Miok Ŏnni, I'm worried about Chagŭn Ŏnni these days. How does she live? They have no money, right?"

She gives me a comforting smile. "They are okay. Don't worry. I send them rice, and they have a little bit of money to get by."

"Did you know Minam Ŏnni told me that Chagŭn Ŏnni and her husband never fight? She said they really love each other, but usually, couples who have money problems fight more easily."

Miok chuckles, "Those two really love each other. They have no money, but they are happy together." Chagŭn Ŏnni and Taehui suddenly appear. We hug and walk toward the taxi rank.

Later that night, as we prepare for our drinking and *anju* session, Chagŭn Ŏnni hugs me and spanks my bum, amused about what I told Miok. "Our Mi Soon! Our pretty Mi Soon. I wish I had pocket money to give you. I'm your older sister, and I'm supposed to give you pocket money. That's how it should be, but I'm embarrassed that I have no money to give you. You always give me money, and you bought me that expensive Teflon fry pan!" She quickly retells the story to Miok about last month's LG Mart shopping trip with Ŏmma and K'ŭn Ŏnni.

Miok clenches her teeth as she hugs and spanks me too. "Our Mi Soon! Our Mi Soon is so nice."

"Both of you are so nice to me! Isn't it fun for the three of us to be together like this?"

Miok finishes preparing our anju. She lays out dried squid with spicy red pepper paste, fresh and still-squirming octopus legs with sesame soy dipping sauce, toasted walnuts, and salty seaweed laver on the table. I pour plum wine with floating, delicate gold flakes into our one-ounce ceramic wine cups. We say *"kŏnbae,"* and gulp down our first shot. A moment of silence lingers after we swallow and dramatically exhale, and I say, "Chagŭn Ŏnni, do you like your Teflon fry pan?"

"I don't know. I haven't used it yet. I put it in a special place. I'll use it when I absolutely need to. I'm saving it for a special day."

pimple

A short walk from my apartment brings me to a very small convenience store, maybe the size of a large walk-in closet. An old couple runs the shop; they must be in their late sixties or early seventies. It's hard to tell how old people are from that generation, because they lived through the colonial period and the war and are often younger than they look.

The husband is more gregarious than his wife, but she warms up after a while. The shop opens early and closes very late, often around three in the morning, and I think it's hard for them to make a living. They sell a lot of random things along with the usual items, but the prices are quite high, especially for dish soap and laundry detergent. Peter and I like to give them our business when we can—we always buy orange juice and bottles of water, and we deposit our extra coins in the tin collection they give to the *halmŏnis* and *halabŏjis* who don't have enough money and who pick up recyclable containers on the streets for extra income.

We are out of water again, and so I run down to the store in my grubby clothes. The ajŏssi is working tonight, watching the small television that sits on the shelf with the potato chips and snack food. I grab the water, but I always feel like I should buy more than that, so I look around for a moment. The hours and days must get long, always staying in the same space, so I think the customers bring energy to him in the same way friendly co-workers create a nice environment for each other.

As I look around the shop, the ajŏssi starts to talk to me, and I feel like he is staring at the large pimple that recently took root on my right cheek. A few days a month, my skin breaks out like I'm pre-pubescent, and I always feel embarrassed about this. I decide to buy some snacks, orange juice, and diet soda, and he totals it all together with the two bottles of water. As he calculates, he looks even more closely at my face. I feel very self-conscious. He says, "Eight thousand wŏn. What's wrong with your face? You look so tired."

"Yes, I am so tired. I've been working too much lately."

"You do look very tired. But what's that, right there?" He actually reaches out to touch my large red pimple.

I immediately step back to gain some personal space. I want to die. I turn bright red, and all I can say is, "It's a pimple." I give him ten thousand wŏn, take the change, and dart out.

A few days later, I walk home from the bus stop. I see their shop, and I think about the new pimple forming on my left cheek. I know we need water, so I brave it and walk in again, hoping for a quick transaction. I try to keep my body at an angle, so he can only see my clear right cheek.

Just before he hands me the change, he starts to point toward my left cheek. Before he can even bring it up, I immediately say, "Yes! Yes, I know. You don't have to tell me. I have a big, red pimple. It's right here. I'm sorry!"

He looks a little surprised. "No. No, not that. I just want to tell you we now have the Polo mints your boyfriend asked about last time." He points to the mints, which are in proximity to my left cheek. I feel foolish, especially because there is another customer in the shop.

I sheepishly smile and say, "Thank you. I'll tell Peter about them," and I run out the door as fast as I can.

Ŏmma

We walk arm in arm down the small alleyway to the local LG Mart. Ŏmma walks with dignity, wearing her full makeup and long black dress, even though she has lived a life of hardship. She is tougher than tough, and she belches and spits like a professional ball player if the moment calls for it. At the tender age of twelve, all Ŏmma dreamed about were books and school, but she had to raise her younger siblings, a sister and two half-brothers, instead of studying every day. After she turned eighteen, her mother forced her to marry the first man who came along. Ŏmma was literally given a blanket and a few items and told to get married quickly; our father was the first man she met. After she got married, she immediately began to have children, and she still had to help raise her younger siblings. For all these reasons, I love and respect her, but I find it harder to become as close to her as I am with my three oldest sisters.

The oppressive sun is shining brightly, and just as we are about to cross the street to get soju and beer for our drinking session tonight, a tiny, frail halmŏni passes us on the right with a cart, burdened with a full load of flattened cardboard boxes that she is taking to some recycling center, where she will receive next to nothing for the weight of the cardboard. The city is full of halmŏnis and halabŏjis who don't receive enough social security to live out their golden years in comfort.

The halmŏni takes a sharp right, heading up a small but steep hill, but she is too weak to push the cart up effectively. Even though Ŏmma suffers from diabetes and her legs are constantly sore and her stomach bloated, as if it were second nature, she puts her purse on her wrist, rolls up her sleeves, grabs the metal bar of the cart, and helps the halmŏni push the unforgiving cart up the toughest part of the hill. The halmŏni gives insa to my mother, and they part ways. It all happens very quickly. Ŏmma pulls her sleeves down, walks back to me, grabs my arm, and leads me across the street to LG Mart—before I can even say a word about her kindness.

fat down

I belong to a large health club in Myeongdong, where there is also a sauna and *tchimjil bang*. Although she isn't related to me at all, I call my sauna ajumma "auntie." She's in her late forties and quite pretty, with delicate, smooth skin and mischievous eyes. I sometimes buy bottled water from her when I work out. There aren't many places in the world where the different women who give you a locker number, sell you water or juice, and give you a facial or massage will see you naked and then soak with you in a large green-tea bath. Maybe this is why my sauna auntie and I have a unique relationship.

Today she grabs my bum for the first time and pats it, saying, "*Uri* Mi Soon, how much do you weigh?"

I say, "I don't know," and before I can stop her, she drags me over to the scale and orders me to get on it. For some reason I obey her like she is my mother.

She reads, "Fifty-five kilos," and then she firmly says, "You must lose five kilos."

"I don't think that's possible or healthy."

"Of course it's healthy. It's what everyone wants! Don't you want that?"

I'm embarrassed at this point, as everyone around us hears my weight and bad Korean, so I say, "Okay, I will try for fifty kilos." She smiles with satisfaction and returns to her station, where she sells everything from bras and panties to shampoo and conditioner sachets, along with all kinds of beverages, including the diet drink Fat Down, which is supposed to increase the fat you burn during a workout.

Even though losing five kilos is nonsense, and I should know better than to listen to her orders, I now feel fatter than usual. I walk over to buy Fat Down from her; it's a small glass bottle with a metal screw cap. I take it back to my locker, and as I open it, hoping to drink it as discreetly as possible while crouched behind my locker door, the metal cap cuts my index finger, and a trickle of blood makes its way down my hand.

Still holding my Fat Down, I run to my sauna auntie to show her my finger. "Uri Mi Soon, come over here." I sit down on a bench, and she brings over some wet and dry tissues along with a small first-aid kit. She tenderly and meticulously cleans my cut, shaking her head back and forth in disappointment, making little *ttut ttut ttut* sounds. She rubs some ointment on the cut and then slowly puts a bandage around my finger. She's still holding my hand, and she looks me in my eyes and says, "You were so excited about losing your five kilos that you opened your Fat Down too quickly! Be careful next time. Slowly . . . open it slowly!" She gently squeezes my hand, kisses the bandage on my finger, spanks my bum, and sends me on my way.

cleaning ajumma

At Korea University's Institute of Foreign Language Studies, the teachers' offices are on the seventh floor. Each floor has its own cleaning ajumma, and our ajumma happens to have one of the most cherubic, childlike, and endearing faces I've ever seen on a human being of any age; she is near seventy.

Both Peter and I greet her daily, and the three of us act as if we are in some kind of mutual admiration society. She can't be more than four-and-a-half-feet tall. She dyes her hair jet black, and it is permed into a tight curl. She wears no makeup, but her skin tone is naturally pink and her eyes are terrifically bright.

I usually have some kind of a conversation with her in the bathroom about little daily things. And even though Peter can't speak much Korean, he manages to have a friendly exchange with her every day through body language and lots of smiles in the hallway, elevator, or when she changes the toilet paper in the men's bathroom. She works hard, cleaning all of our offices daily and keeping the bathroom as clean as a new hospital.

This December, Peter's classes end before mine, and he is already traveling abroad, waiting for me to join him. Today our cleaning ajumma pulls me aside after I wash my hands. "Do you know today is my last day?" she asks.

"No. I had no idea. Why are you leaving?"

"I turn seventy next January, and I'm being forced to retire. I don't want to, though. I like it here, and I still need the money."

"I'm sorry. I will miss you. I like seeing you every day."

"Me too, and I must tell you that your boyfriend is very nice. I want to say goodbye to him, too, but haven't seen him lately."

I tell her that Peter is abroad and won't be back until next March. We share hugs, and I feel sad knowing I won't see her again.

A few months later, Peter is back, and we are in our neighborhood laughing and talking as we walk to our bus stop. As we turn the corner, I see a tiny halmŏni holding a plastic bag, shuffling along, trying not to slip on the little patches of dirty ice. It takes about ten seconds for it all to register. All three of us stop in slow motion with our mouths open, displaying the biggest grins on our faces. It is our seventh-floor cleaning ajumma!

She walks up to us, and we try to catch our breaths, entirely surprised at this chance meeting. I switch into Korean and ask her how she is doing. She's well and is visiting her friend who lives here. She asks if we live in the neighborhood, too. I nod, and then she turns to Peter, speaking only in Korean but looking at him tenderly. "I didn't get to say goodbye to you, and I felt sad about it. I wanted to thank you for all the times you gave me little presents and holiday money. You are a kind, handsome man. I am so pleased to meet you now." I act as their interpreter; Peter says kind things to her as well.

I hug her and wish her the best. All three of us know the chances of seeing each other again are slim to none, and that it wouldn't make sense for us to plan to meet, either. She makes eye contact with Peter, opening her small frail arms for him, and although he is about a foot-and-a-half taller than she, he gently sweeps down to hug her—like a grown son would hug his mother.

xylitol gum

A man with cerebral palsy in a motorized wheelchair makes his way down the subway car aisle. Most of the people ignore him or avoid eye contact. He has a handsome head of black hair and must be in his mid-thirties. He's selling Xylitol, a Korean brand of gum that usually costs five hundred wŏn in the convenience stores, but he charges one thousand wŏn per pack. He wears a large laminated sign that tells his story and why he's selling the gum.

Coins, bills, and small green packs of gum are mixed together in a navy blue drawstring bag that sits on his lap. I pull out a thousand-wŏn bill to buy a pack of gum, and he flashes a friendly smile while struggling to say, "Thank you." I tell him I'd like to buy another, and his eyes light up a bit.

An end seat right next to the exit door opens up, so I grab it. As I'm about to open my Xylitol, the man wheels up to the sliding door that will take him into the next subway car. He has a hard time reaching the handle to slide it over, so I pop up to open the heavy door along with the door to the connecting car. At this point, people are staring at us in a way that is neither kind nor rude, so we give a quick insa and I walk back to my seat; it's now occupied by a middle-aged Korean businessman wearing a smart suit. The second he sees me he stands up, giving me my seat back, but I motion to him to stay seated. By the way he kindly insists I sit back down, I know he saw me open the sliding doors. I take my seat back as we exchange a friendly smile, and he stands in front of the subway exit door, right next to where I am sitting. I open the pack of Xylitol and give him a piece, and we both unwrap our gum, popping it into our mouths at the same time.

Now the man in the wheelchair is stuck and needs to be lifted a bit, so he can get into the next subway car. Two men get up from their seats to help him through, and the subway comes to a halt at Euljiro-3-ga.[12] The businessman and I continue to chew our gum as we glance at the man wheeling his way down the next subway car. We exchange genuine smiles, and the man in the smart business suit walks out the subway door.

six-hour norae bang

We are in Hongdae.[13] Joanne loves the ten-thousand-wŏn shopping bargains, and we're drawn to a sales rack outside that has a strange array of dresses. I hate buying this stuff because I usually never wear it, but we both spot a black, cotton, cherry-print strapless dress. We grab it, hold it up, and say it would look cute on each other. Finding only one on the rack, we walk in the store and stumble across a navy blue, polyester miniskirt with overall straps. It's weird, but for some reason we think it might look cute with the right shirt; we bargain the two dresses down to thirty thousand wŏn.

We stop at a Buy The Way convenience store and stock up on eight cans of Prime beer, because Joanne's dad's doctor says it's the only Korean beer that doesn't use formaldehyde as a preservative. After we hide our Prime in our bags, nestled under our dresses, we go into a basement norae bang next door to the dress shop. Once in our private room, we begin to punch in our regular songs: Whitney

Houston's "Saving All My Love," Skid Row's "I Remember You," Peter Cetera's "Glory of Love," Britney Spears's "Toxic," 50 Cent's "In Da Club," and the list goes on and on. Although we only paid for an hour, there is usually an hour of *sŏbisŭ*, or extra time that's free. The amount of songs we enter will take up at least two hours.

I take the mike and, halfway through, as I'm belting out *No other woman is going to treat you right—because tonight is the night—I'm feeling all right—we'll be making love the whole night through,* Joanne grabs the two dresses and two cans of Prime.

At the end of the song, we say "kŏnbae," and she throws the cherry-print dress on my lap saying, "Let's try them on!" We begin to change, and as we are pulling up our dresses, with our pants around our ankles, someone knocks and opens the door. We yelp, slam the door, hide our Prime, and pull up our pants under our dresses. With red and embarrassed faces, we open the door to a teenage boy. He looks flustered as he walks in. He sets a plate of cherry tomatoes and shrimp-flavored potato chips on the coffee table between us and says, "Enjoy this."

As he leaves the room, we say, "Please give us a lot of sŏbisŭ!" He nods his head and leaves as quickly as he can. The beer keeps flowing, and we punch in songs like professionals. Our two hours are up, but we aren't ready to leave. We order extra time in fifteen-minute increments, singing each number like it's our last. We are still wearing our dress-and-pants combos, and while Joanne is belting out *I'm toxic—you're toxic—I'm slipping under,* we experience buyer's remorse: The navy blue dress is stupid and ugly, and we hope to return it right after our session is finished.

Every time the boy gives us an extra fifteen minutes, we scream into our microphones, "*Kamsa hamnida*. Please give us more sŏbisŭ!"

By the time we sing *I just want someone I can talk to—I love you just the way you are,* our throats are sore and voices are cracking. We have lost all track of time, and our song timer is back down to three minutes. We check the time on our cell phones and are shocked to find that we've been in this tiny, bathroom-size singing box for six hours. We decide we have to respect all this sŏbisŭ the teenage boy has given us and pull it together for our final song, "Livin' on a Prayer." Giving it all we've got, watching the time tick down to one minute, we scream out *Take my hand, we'll make it I swear . . .* The teenage boy puts another fifteen minutes on the timer.

Joanne looks at me. "I can't do it. I just can't do it."

"Me neither. We gotta go and try to get our money back for this dress."

We change as quickly as we can and then run out to the front. "Thank you so much for all the time, but we have to return this ugly dress before it's too late."

He blushes. We give insa and run up the stairs to find the store closed.

help me!

We have just devoured two large, crunchy Asian pears, and the peelings lay lifeless and brown on the small floor table in front of my parents. Ŏmma is leaning against the industrial-size refrigerator, and Appa is in front of the three-drawer kimch'i refrigerator. I stand in front of them with my arms in the starting taekwondo stance. "Are you ready?"

With great enthusiasm and a deep, hoarse voice, Appa says, "We're ready."

"I'm going to do the yellow-belt form first." It's a sunny autumn afternoon, and the door to their home is open; a light breeze drifts in, and I begin to move with as much strength and precision as I can.

I use a good part of the main room as I move through the form, and Appa keeps shouting out, "Handsome! So handsome!"

I move on to the harder blue-belt form, the one I'm learning these days, and now take up all the space in the room, coming very close to them as I do a right-leg–left-leg kicking sequence that ends above their heads. As I finish this form, they clap their hands with delight. Ŏmma says, "Our Mi Soon is nice and strong!"

Appa stands up to show me a few moves, and then his face becomes very serious. He says, "Mi Soon-ah, you must use your taekwondo if a bad man is trying to attack you!" Although he is seventy, he doesn't look frail. He looks uneven, like he's had a rough life, but his arms still have little strong muscles. "Do you know what you should say if you are being attacked?"

"What?"

"*Towa chuseyo!*' You must say it loudly . . . Promise me you will yell it loudly. And then give him your strong side kick and run, yelling, 'Towa chuseyo!'"

"Okay."

"Do it now. I want to see you practice it."

"Right now?" Appa nods his head, and Ŏmma says go ahead.

I stand back up, give a strong right side kick, and then run around the room, just as Appa did, yelling, "Towa chuseyo!"

He isn't satisfied with my enthusiasm, so he stands up to do it with me. He yells, "Louder! Say it louder, Mi Soon-ah!"

"Towa chuseyo! Towa chuseyo!" We run around the room, screaming this at the top of our lungs, throwing little side kicks every few steps, and Ŏmma sits on the floor, clapping and smiling.

seaweed chips

I'm late, but I've got to make it to the American embassy today to get some extension pages in my passport, so I can receive my Chinese visa by this weekend. I put my arm out for a taxi. The cab stops, and for no special reason I hop in the front, contrary to the advice of my sisters, who warned me always to sit in the back of the cab in case I need to get away from a psycho driver.

I notice the taxi driver is at least seventy, quite a bit older than the average middle-aged drivers in Seoul, and he is very small and frail. His face resembles a corrugated walnut shell. It seems like he can barely see over the dashboard. I ask him to take me to the American embassy, explaining that I'm a little late. He kindly says he will take the fastest route there.

There's always traffic in Seoul, and as we wait at a stoplight, he takes out a little plastic container that fits perfectly in the palm of his hand. He opens it slowly; it contains a wooden toothpick and small, deep-fried, sugar-coated seaweed chips. He uses the toothpick to eat two seaweed chips, tightly closes the lid, and puts the container snug under the emergency brake. We finally get our green light and are on our way, but then we are stopped again at another long red light. He goes through the same ritual again, only eating one seaweed chip this time. This continues at all the lights as we laboriously make our way down Jogno Street.[14]

At the fifth light, he moves the container closer to me. "Would you like one?" he asks.

"No. No. I'm fine."

He continues, "My wife packs these for me every day because I suddenly quit smoking three months ago. It is very hard to do, so anytime I want to smoke I eat these."

I ask him how much he used to smoke, and he says almost three packs a day. He starts to ask me questions about where I'm from, which happens every time I take a taxi, but I don't mind telling him my whole adoption saga. His driving is a bit unsteady, like his shaky voice, and it makes me a tad nervous, but I continue to answer his stream of questions, because there is friendly energy in the smoke-free air.

On his dashboard I notice a small, four-inch plastic statue that's black and white and resembles a totem pole; it has an angry face, and its body bobs back and forth because it's mounted on some kind of a spring. I ask him what it is, and he says, "If I don't want to eat my snack, and I want to smoke, I look at this scary guy, and he yells at me not to smoke." He continues in a solemn voice, "I'm very scared of him." He points his finger at the statue, giving it an angry look, staring it down as if the statue is a real person about to confront him. I laugh a little, but his tone tells me not to. "Because of this scary guy and my seaweed chips, I've been able to quit smoking. I smoked my whole life, but even stopping for three months has improved my health."

As we approach the back of the US embassy, we both gasp at the long line of people that wraps around one side of the building and ends in the back, well into the streets. It's still morning, and he and I both realize that the line is full of Koreans waiting in the already scorching sun for their interviews to receive visas to the States. "You have an American passport, right?" I nod my head, and he pulls the car up to one of the Korean security police who is keeping order in the line. He rolls down the window on my side and asks where the Americans enter.

The policeman says, "But . . . She's not American. This is her line," pointing to the line of hot and exhausted Koreans.

My taxi driver says, "Oh, yes she is. She is American. She was adopted to America when she was three months old, but she met her birth family a few years ago. That is why she looks Korean and can't speak our language."

The man gives us a vacant nod while pointing to the front of the building. The taxi driver takes off quickly, rushing me to the front of the US embassy, where there is a line of only five people. He says, "Now, this is much better for you, right?" He smiles at me as I get out of the car. I wait in the short line, watching him stare down his statue, eat one more seaweed chip, and drive away.

pupster

Joanne and I enter the black gate to my duplex. "Hey, Pupster! Mi Soon, will you call him Pupster? Please?"

"No. That's stupid, but I feel bad for that dog. He just sits there all day long on that short chain. Why don't they walk him? It's annoying and mean of them, but they're nice people."

As we walk into the shared entryway, we insa to the halmŏni and halabŏji. Later that day, when we leave the house, Joanne says, "Bye, Pupster. I like that name. Please call him Pupster!"

"No . . . Okay. I'll think about it." I wave goodbye to the scrawny Jindeok[15] dog.

A month later, Peter says, "Mi Soon, did you notice one of our neighbors is missing?"

"No. Who? Is it the halmŏni? Is she in the hospital?"

"Think about it, what day was yesterday?"

"I don't know. Tell me."

"It was one of the *bongnal* days."

"Oh my god! Are you serious? Did they eat Pupster?"

"Who's Pupster?"

"Oh, Joanne gave him that name."

"Well, I think Pupster was someone's dinner yesterday. Maybe it's for the better . . . he lived a dreadful existence."

"Sad! I can't believe it. Maybe they ate Pupster. I'm gonna ask them."

The next day I see the owner of the home. "Halabŏji," I ask, "By chance, did you eat your dog yesterday?"

He chuckles deeply and slowly. "Ha—ha—ha. No, I didn't eat that dog."

"Well, where is it then?"

"Some man came by and said he wanted to take care of the dog. And I don't need it. We just found it and gave it a place to sleep and food to eat."

"I still think someone ate him yesterday because of bongnal. Sad!"

Halabŏji, with his dark, friendly eyes and long, coarse gray eyebrows—almost as long as window awnings—chuckles a little more, like the way he does when he watches American pro wrestling. "Don't worry. I don't think they ate it. They just wanted to take it with them."

"I don't know. I think someone ate him." He smiles and walks back into his home. I am not a dog or cat lover; I never interacted with Pupster directly, but for the next few weeks, every time I go in or out—looking at his empty wooden house—I feel a little lump in my throat.

ponytail

The subway door opens. There isn't any place to sit, so I stand in front of a father and his two children, a girl and boy about the ages of ten and seven, respectively. Their father stands up to move between them and stop their bickering. He gives them a playful smile, but he looks exhausted and nods off between subway stops. A seat opens up next to the little girl, and I grab it.

The little girl is chubby, by Korean standards. She has a big face—something that living in Korea has made me notice, sadly—and she wears her long, thick black hair high up in a ponytail. I think how lucky she is to have that shiny black head of hair—so healthy that the bottom of her ponytail is as thick as the top.

As the subway rocks us back and fourth, her ponytail lightly brushes my bare left arm. I don't know why, but I like how it feels, ticklish and endearing; maybe because I wish my hair wasn't so short and damaged from the hack job at Parisienne.

The little boy taps the father's thighs, and he wakes. I read my book, but I pay attention to them as well. From the corner of my eye, I can see the little girl trying to decipher the paragraphs of English as I turn the pages. As she does this, she pulls out her hair binder and her hair falls down, covering her shoulders and back, framing her plump face. She runs her fingers through her hair, trying to put her ponytail back in. Failing at this, she turns to her father. "Daddy, can you fix my hair?"

He stares at her with a blank and almost scared look. "I don't know how to do that." He half-heartedly grabs the binder, and I see the wheels turning in his head as he tries to figure out how his wife might do it.

I turn to the little girl and, with my best Korean pronunciation, ask, "Do you want Ŏnni to do it for you?" She picks up a trace of accent in my voice, but she lends me an innocent smile, handing me her hair tie and turning her back to me. The father looks relieved and nods off again.

I use my fingers to comb it out, and I begin to draw up her massive amount of hair at the crown of her head, but I can't get all the bumps and ridges out. I wish I had a comb. I start again and make it as smooth as I can. I can tell she enjoys this attention from me, like I'm her older cousin doing her hair in her bedroom, except we don't know each other and are simply riding the subway together. When I finish, she gives me a little insa and says, "Thank you."

Her father is fully awake now. "Did you thank your Ŏnni?" he asks. She says yes, but she bows again, thanking me once more.

I return to my book, and they exit at the next subway stop. As she walks to the right, hand in hand with her father, I can see her looking for me through the subway window, but I'm blocked by the people who have just entered the car. I try to move my head to the right and left so she can see me, but it doesn't work. A moment before the subway takes off, they walk by the next door on the right, and she peers in to see me smiling at her. She gives me a huge smile and energetically waves goodbye; I wave back the second before the door closes.

cable ajŏssi

I press the button, and a loud *buzz* sound opens the gate. A man wearing the humid heat on his damp t-shirt meets me at the top of the stairs. He notices my strange accent immediately, but he doesn't acknowledge it, so I feel relieved. He speaks in fast Korean, explaining that he's going to drill a hole through the window frame for the gray cable line. I say, "I understand," but the only thing on my mind is trying to formulate the Korean sentences I need to say next. "Sir, I'm sorry. Outside. Under the table, a small, baby bird died yesterday. I am strange. Since I was child, I hate dead animals. Please throw the bird away outside."

He looks at me with confusion as I point to the bird under my white plastic table, and now he looks at me with revulsion, "I don't want to touch it either."

I beg him, "I'm so sorry, but I hate dead animals. Strange feeling. Please." I walk to him, saying, "Here are little plastic bags for your hands." He says okay and asks for some newspaper. I feel thankful.

Thirty seconds later he walks in the door and tries to hand me the dead bird wrapped in paper. "NOOOOO! *Aniyo!* Go outside please. Take it outside, please!" Now it's truly confirmed that I'm a freak. As he walks down the stairs, I yell, "Thank you, Ajössi! Thank you!"

He finishes installing the cable, and I can tell he doesn't know how to react to me, but he is kind. I give him two leftover cans of Prime beer that Joanne and I bought for the norae bang but didn't drink. He says, "Thank you, I will enjoy them," and gives insa as he leaves my home.

oxy clean

I am outside, on my knees, sporting my Michael Jackson mask. I've got a bottle of Oxy Clean, Korean Windex, clenched tightly in my right hand. I must sanitize the area where the baby bird died. I am spraying constantly, as if trying to put out a small campfire, and I'm wrapped up in my own world.

In the midst of my trance I hear Joanne's scream. "Stop it! The Oxy is getting in my eyes! The fan is blowing it in my eyes, and the whole house smells!"

"Sorry, man, but I gotta get this clean." I walk back in the house, and she looks up at me in disbelief with sore, red eyes. Again I say, "Sorry."

Later in the afternoon I'm sitting on my Muji floor chair, and I see two large birds land on my white plastic table. It makes me nervous. I really hate birds. As I pound on the window, I scream at the birds, *"Ka, ka! Bballi ka!"* A minute later, it hits me that those were the baby bird's parents! How sad. The parents were looking for their lost baby bird, when just a few hours ago the cable ajŏssi wrapped their baby in my *International Herald Tribune* and placed it in the garbage bin, right outside my black front gate.

love motel

My class of three students, who originally signed up for an Effective Speaking class, has taken on a life of its own. We seem only to have group discussions in coffee shops and go on field trips around Seoul. It's an eclectic mix of three: Young Sook is in her early forties, and she's an MBA student at Kodae; Yeon Hwa is in her early thirties, and she is preparing for the teaching licensure exam; Jong Suk is in his early twenties, and he's planning to study abroad for his PhD in macroeconomics.

We always have interesting conversations about Korean society. During one field trip, when it was only the two women and me, we delved into the depressing topic of beauty and its benefits in Korean society. Lovely Yeon Hwa said, "When you hear 'you're ugly' in young age, you study hard to be success and then make a lot of money and then get plastic surgery. It's a trend these days." She joked and laughed about the last part, but there was a certain amount of truth to what she said.

I asked them if beauty was the most important thing for a Korean man when he searches for a partner. Young Sook said, "First, a man wants a girl with a beautiful face. As he is older, he wants a girl with a beautiful body. Finally, he wants a nice girl." The three of us continued the conversation and lamented about the superficiality of it all; we bonded over the pressure we feel, even at our age, to be beautiful in Korea.

Today, Jong Suk is able to join our field trip. He is a bulky, strong young man who is very kind-hearted and pragmatic. We go to Deoksu Palace, near City Hall. Even though it is pouring—as it has for the past three weeks because of typhoon season—we enjoy the solitude that can only exist in this public place because of the weather. We can't get over how peaceful, nice, and inexpensive (at only a thousand-wŏn entrance fee) this place is. Seoul is expensive these days.

After an hour in the rain, we're hungry and decide on k'alguksu, one of the best kinds of food to eat on a rainy or cold day. The four of us hop in a cab to a famous noodle restaurant near Gyeongbuk Palace, a large palace near Insadong and Gwanghwamun. Since we are one of the first tables seated, and the restaurant isn't quite open, we put in our order but must wait a bit. We begin to chat about what makes a successful marriage, since Yeon Hwa and Young Sook are both married. I mention how long my parents in Minnesota have been happily married and that, when I was younger, they used to go on regular dates to dinner and a movie while my sister, brother, and I were left with a babysitter.

bravo your life!

My students are surprised. Often, in Korean society, after the children arrive, dates and private time for the parents end. Since Young Sook has been with her husband for twenty-something years, and she has two almost-grown children, I ask her, "Do you and your husband go on dates?" I expect her to say no, that her husband is too busy with their international jewelry company, or that they go to church together. But to my surprise, she says, "Yes! We go on dates all the time. I love going on dates!"

Yeon Hwa claps her hands and gives Young Sook a satisfied smile. She continues, "Do you know where my favorite place for a date is?" We remain silent, waiting for her to tell us. "I love going to the love motel. We do it regularly. Do you guys know about the love motel? It's such a nice place to go. My husband really likes it."

All three of us become awkwardly silent, truly not knowing what to say next, so we just nod our heads and smile. As I try to erase the image of Young Sook in an hourly love motel with her husband, Jong Suk says, "Yep! That's a place. That's a place to go. Yep! That's a very nice place to go."

I'm about to change the subject when four steaming-hot bowls of knife-cut noodles arrive and are placed in front of us. We immediately grab our chopsticks, stare into our bowls, and begin to eat.

double eyelids

I sit soaking in a hot green-tea bath. I'm at the *mogyok t'ang* by my birth parents' home, but I'm on my own. There is an ajumma in her forties who has been in the bath as long as I have, and I notice her staring at my face. I begin to feel paranoid, like I have something coming out of my nose. I check my face, smile, and give her a small bow, which she takes as an invitation to come over to me.

A white towel around my head holds my hair in and frames my face. She sits as close as she can, right next to me; her leg touches mine. She says, "How old are you?"

"I'm twenty-nine."

"Are you married?"

"No, not yet."

"You better hurry! You are running out of time." If I hear this one more time I think I will jump in front of a train, but I just calmly nod my head, hoping she will leave or at least not talk to me anymore. Since this mogyok t'ang is small, and there is nowhere else for me to go except out, I remain close to her.

She begins to examine my face closely, and I feel weird. "You are pretty. You have a small face. That's very important." I feel self-conscious and don't say a word. "But . . . if you just had the double-eyelid surgery, you would be much prettier."

In my best Korean accent, I say, "No. I don't ever want that kind of surgery or any surgery."

Her three ajumma friends emerge from the sauna and join us. Since Seoul is so crowded, private space in public does not exist. She asks them to look at my face, and would I not be so much prettier if I had the double-eyelid surgery. They move in closer. I feel trapped and want to leave, but the four of them have me surrounded. The leader of the ajumma gang begins to lift my eyelids up and down to show the other ajummas the before and after look. "See? Look how much prettier she would be if she had that surgery. It doesn't take long, and it's very cheap." They smile at me expectantly, waiting for me to say something.

I don't care that I just got here: It's time for me to leave. I painfully smile and stand up. "It's hot in here. I've got to go, but okay, I'll get the double-eyelid surgery."

They clap their hands victoriously, like they just won an important match. I walk out into the cold locker room and dry myself off, staring closely at my face in the mirror.

photo shoot

It's Sunday. Minam, her husband Sewon, Chagŭn Ŏnni, and I are lying around on the floor in the main room of our parents' home. We are waiting for K'ŭn Ŏnni to come home from church so we can go to her house for lunch. Chagŭn Ŏnni is sprawled out on the floor, tired as usual, semi-sleeping, and barely contributing to the conversation.

Minam walks to her purse, takes out a small makeup tube, and says to Ŏmma and me, "Do you know about BB crème?" She doesn't wait for us to reply. "It does three things. It's foundation, sunscreen, and a skin whitener . . . and very expensive. Sewon *Oppa* bought it for me today." She stands in front of the large hanging mirror and old dresser that has a red rice cooker and a large wooden makeup box on top of it, and she applies the BB crème liberally to her face with happiness and pride.

Sometimes I can't believe what a princess my fourth sister can be. She is only three years older than I am, and she barely made it into the generation that began to benefit from Korea's newfound prosperity. I try to understand where she is coming from, knowing that she loves our family but wants to define herself as different as she continues to secure her position in the Korean middle class. As she rubs in the BB crème, Minam tells all of us about her new leather furniture, which Sewon Oppa also bought recently.

Chagŭn Ŏnni looks sad and asks, "What was wrong with your old furniture?"

"Nothing. I just wanted to change the atmosphere in our home. And the leather sofa looks great, doesn't it, Oppa?"

Sewon is a quiet man, and he just nods his head. Minam goes on with her bragging, while Chagŭn Ŏnni begins to quickly shut down. She stands up, drags herself into the other bedroom, and lies down on the heated floor with her back to us and the door wide open.

The phone rings and we get the okay to head to K'ŭn Ŏnni's house, a three-minute walk from our parents' home. Everyone gets ready to walk out the door, but Chagŭn Ŏnni stays on the floor; she ignores everyone. We can't convince her to leave with us, so we finally just go.

As we walk to K'ŭn Ŏnni's house, Minam links her arm with mine and says, "The reason Chagŭn Ŏnni is acting like that is because she hears what I say about my good husband, and her husband can't ever buy her anything. They have no money." I feel irritated with Minam, and I ask her why she has to brag in front of Chagŭn Ŏnni when we all know they barely have enough food to eat. Minam becomes petulant. "I don't care about their money problems anymore. We loaned them ten million wŏn a couple years ago for a business Chagŭn Ŏnni's husband was going to start. The business failed, and he never paid us back."

"Still, you don't need to talk about expensive things in front of her; it makes her feel bad." Minam ignores what I say.

Later that afternoon we are back at our parents' home, lying on the floor again, snacking on fruit. Chagŭn Ŏnni is in better spirits, and I take her and my small makeup bag into the bathroom. I tell her that even though I don't have a lot of products in the bag, I'm going to do her makeup beautifully. She tells me that she has no reason to wear makeup, but I insist. She crouches next to the water faucet that stands about a foot above the tiled floor and brusquely washes her face with a bar of Dove soap. She stands next to the window as I apply something similar to BB crème (minus the whitening agent) to her face, along with blush, eye shadow, and lipstick. She tells me my crème smells good and must be expensive. With guilt, I admit that it is a little expensive, but she smiles and hugs me. After her makeup I style her hair, and I can feel how she enjoys being doted on by me. When I was a little girl, I used to always do my American mother's hair; pampering people is still a hobby of mine.

We leave the bathroom to find everyone playing cards, watching TV, or sleeping. A few people in our family notice Chagŭn Ŏnni and compliment her. She smiles shyly.

She looks really nice. I tell her to put on my light blue blazer so we can go outside to take a few pictures with my small digital camera. I position her on the steps, making her pose different ways as if I'm a professional fashion photographer, and she listens to me as if she is a top supermodel.

After about thirty shots, I'm happy with the results; I show her all of them. She smiles and laughs, something I rarely see or hear from her. As Chagŭn Ŏnni takes off my jacket, I tell her I will send her the best photos.

We are tired, so we take a quick nap. When I wake up, Taehui, her seven-year-old son, is taking more photos of everyone with my digital camera, and I don't mind because I showed him how to do it last time I was with him.

Later that night, I want to show Peter the pictures from our photo shoot. I turn the camera on to find all of the pictures mistakenly erased.

penguin man

In Myeongdong, from the late afternoon into the night, sellers stand behind their large street carts offering a variety of things: Ttŏkbokki, squid cooked and cut various ways, panties, stuffed animals, socks, knock-off designer sunglasses, and even clothes for your lap dog. The cart owners range in age from the young and hip to the weary and middle-aged. They work long and tiring hours, and during lunch and dinner time they can be spotted crouched down behind their carts, huddled over big bowls of noodles or rice delivered from a nearby restaurant.

Then there are the sellers who don't own carts; they bring their products in large rolling "grow" bags, which can grow (with the right unzipping) as tall as an elementary student. One of these sellers works along one of Myeongdong's major streets. He is always there. He sells only a few things: four blue plastic penguins that are magnetically attached to each other and are battery operated, a plastic scuba diver that continuously "swims" into the wall of a small orange plastic tub of water, and a very small remote-control-operated car that zips through the feet of all the people who pass by. The penguins waddle all day long, making a squeaking sound as they zigzag their way around. Their owner doesn't seem to care that they bump into the passing feet.

Myeongdong is filled with everything that is young, loud and youthful north of the Han River, and most shops abuse your eardrums with the latest K-pop blaring out their front doors. If it's not pop music vying for your attention, then it's the God-loving Christians who stand on the corners singing hymns in front of a sign that's written in Korean, English, Japanese, and Chinese: *Lord Jesus Heaven. No Jesus Hell.* In the midst of all of this, the cart owners bellow their latest bargains at the top of their lungs, and some even try to drag customers over to look at their goods. But the penguin man doesn't say a word. He is busy driving the small car around his penguins.

Around closing time, the cart owners stack up their goods, wrap them in a large tarp, secure it with a thick rubber bungee cord, and push their cart to a designated area that I've never seen. At eleven o'clock, the penguin man still seems content playing with his toys and smiling at his penguins. I have yet to see him sell anything, and he might even be sad to let a penguin go.

bus fight

Seoul has over twelve million residents, and hundreds of buses wind their way through crowded city streets daily. I'm on a bus back to my house in Pyeongchangdong. Joanne is south of the Han River, but I'm bored and want to hang out with her.

She answers my phone call with an annoyed tone. "What do you want?"

"Would it kill you to say hello to me?"

"I said what do you want?"

"Oh my god. Why are you so mean?"

"I'm not mean. You are!"

"Where are you?"

"I'm waiting for a bus."

"Come over. Let's hang out."

"No!"

"What are you doing today?"

"Not much. I gotta go!"

"Wait! Don't hang up on me!"

"I said I gotta go!"

"Don't you hang up on me. Don't you dare!"

"Shut up! My bus is here." As I stare forward, guess who boards my bus? Joanne Kim! She doesn't see me because I'm sitting toward the back. "I hate talking on the phone when I ride the bus. I'm hanging up now!"

As she walks toward the back of the bus, I say, "You better not hang up on me!" I can see her face—she is annoyed and frustrated. Joanne reaches my seat, and I punch her as hard as I can in her stomach. She screams loudly, having no clue what just happened. When she sees me, we begin to scream with joy and laughter.

jenny

Jenny is a student of mine. She is being raised by her single mother, a nursing professor. From what I can gather, her father was lazy and incompetent, and while Jenny's mother completed her PhD in the States, he just watched TV and played computer games—at least that's what Jenny tells me.

Korea is a judgmental society, with little room to exist comfortably if you don't fit into the norm, and I'm very impressed with how well Jenny's mother raises her. She loves Jenny so much, but in order for her to earn tenure she must work long hours, which means Jenny is enrolled in our English language program at Kodae every weekday, along with a plethora of other hagwŏns.

I don't know why, but I love this little girl, and I worry about her a lot. Her English is advanced, but it's also funny, because her intonation is that of a middle-aged children's librarian, even though she is so tiny and small. She once told me, "Mi Soon, I never really learned Korean or English the right way, because I lived in America when I should have learned only one language."

The first time I taught her she was in second grade, and I noticed that the other children in class thought she was a little weird because her English was so advanced. Jenny sometimes translated things, so the students tolerated her. Now I teach her again; she is already in fourth grade, but this time it's obvious that she has a hard time making friends. She is quite immature for her age, and she still speaks like an excited middle-aged woman, so students roll their eyes or just ignore her. I worry she has no friends at her regular school, either.

She really likes Peter, and she always puts "your" in front of his name when she talks about him. Her mother told me she even writes about Peter and me in her journal. One time our class was trying to figure out a scheduling conflict, and no one could come up with a good alternative. Jenny finally said, "Mi Soon, I think you better ask your Peter later tonight, because everyone knows two brains thinking about something together is the better answer, and I sure think you and your Peter have good brains."

I arrange with Jenny's mother, with whom I've become quite close, to take Jenny out on Sunday afternoon. She drops Jenny off at my house, and it's touching how close they are and how much they love each other. I tell her about our plans for an afternoon movie and a trip to the Cheonggyechon,[16] and we wave as she drives off to work some extra hours at her office.

Jenny and I hop onto a bus, and although I know Jenny feels comfortable with me, this is the first time we will spend an extended period of time alone together. She has her hair tied back in a long ponytail, and she isn't wearing her headgear, the latest addition to her life that makes her feel even more awkward. "Jenny, why aren't you wearing your headgear?"

"I told my mommy that I just don't want to wear it today," she says as she looks down at her lap and fidgets with her fake Chanel cell phone case. I'm reminded of her reaction in our last class, when we were watching *Charlie and the Chocolate Factory*. A young Willy Wonka took off his Halloween ghost costume, uncovering his massive headgear, and Jenny sank down deep into her chair. With her hands touching her headgear, she turned around to look at me with so much innocent embarrassment that I couldn't help but lovingly laugh.

All I could say was, "Your headgear is much better and smaller, very modern!"

As we sit comfortably in the air-conditioned bus, Jenny speaks loudly, and people stare at the two Korean-looking people speaking English. I can tell she feels slightly awkward, and after five minutes she takes out her cell phone, which is used only to call her mother, and begins to play a Korean pop song, norae bang style, with the lyrics displayed as the song plays. Many Koreans use songs as their ring tones, so everyone keeps staring at her, wondering why she won't answer her phone, while she gently sways back and forth to the cheesy melody.

"Is that your favorite song?"

"Oh no, Mi Soon. No. No. It's just the only song I have. I play it when I feel bored."

I tell her we'll be there soon, and we hold hands while she leans on my shoulder. We are on the last stretch of the route when I notice a huge, significantly raised rectangular scar on her left knee. I remember a while ago when she fell. "Jenny, oh my gosh. That scar is so big. Does it hurt?"

"Oh no, Mi Soon. It doesn't hurt, but the doctor wants to do *soosool* there. And my mommy says, 'No way!'"

"Jenny, do you know that the English word for soosool is *surgery*? What kind of surgery?"

She pauses a moment, taking in the new word, and then says, "You see, Mi Soon, they want to take my butt skin and put it right here on my knee. Isn't that crazy? My *butt* skin!"

I laugh loudly at the way she says this, still using her old-lady voice. "Wow. Your butt skin. That is kind of crazy, Jenny. You are so funny."

"What the . . . ? Mi Soon, I just don't know what you are talking about." Our bus arrives at Lotte Department Store in Myeongdong; I grab her hand, and we step down from the bus with our arms linked—like best friends.

mogi bites

We sit on the floor in the main room of my Korean parents' home. We just finished a fast meal with them, inhaling and slurping up their food. I'm pretty used to their ways by now, but sometimes it's still strange eating with them. Because of the soju my father thinks of me as a baby, and sometimes he tears up a small fried fish with his fingers, getting rid of the bones, and stuffs it in my mouth. He has to go to work now, but he's happy we could eat together.

It's a hot summer afternoon, and one reason I hate the summer so much in Seoul is the *mogis*—they are absolutely unbearable to me. My bites swell up, resembling red golf balls, and then itch for days on end. Peter's mogi bites are just little red bumps, but mine are remarkable.

When my sisters are around, there is always lively and colorful conversation, but now it's just Ŏmma, Peter, and me. We have already covered all the basic topics I can talk about in Korean, so we sit, nod, and smile. Peter, with his limited Korean, says *masissŏyo* a couple more times, and

bravo your life!

Ŏmma smiles and claps her hands, happy that Peter thinks her food is delicious.

We sit around the wooden floor table, which my mother just disinfected with a splash of my father's soju, and she cuts small yellow melons for dessert. I see a blue bottle of aerosol mogi killer on the shelf, and I tell Peter about the time Joanne and I stayed overnight and there was one mogi flying around that we couldn't kill. Chagŭn Ŏnni took the can and literally sprayed every part of the room for at least sixty seconds straight, while Joanne and I wheezed ourselves to sleep that night.

As I scratch at the mogi bites all over my arms and legs, he says to me, "Maybe you should ask your mom if she has some traditional remedy for them."

My eyes light up. "Yeah, she's originally from the countryside. Maybe she has some kind of natural herb formula or something!" I show her the bites, and since I don't know how to say in Korean that they itch, I scratch them and tell her they hurt.

She motions to Peter to hand her something on the shelf, and with a puzzled look he points to the can of mogi spray. My mother nods her head, and he hands it to her. She takes the can and tells me to come sit next to her. I give Peter a scared look that says, "What is happening?"

My mother vigorously begins to spray the mogi bites on my arms and legs. We inhale the aerosol cloud that fills the room.

I look at Peter helplessly, my mother looks at my mogi bites with satisfaction, and Peter looks at me with remorse. "Sorry. I guess she just spot-sprayed your mogi bites with some Raid-style repellent."

My mother takes in the surprised looks on our faces, and she laughs. "Mi Soon-ah, your mogi bites don't hurt anymore. Right?"

miss yang & mr. kim

Space is at such a premium in Seoul that on weekends, most public parks are as crowded as supermarkets. I am surprised at how peaceful this small palace park is; there are less than a handful of people here. I walk up a set of stone stairs, and behind the palace is a gravel soccer pitch and a little exercise station, which is common in public nature areas in Korea. I do a few sit-ups and push-ups, check out the palace from above, and walk back down. At the front entrance, there is a little circular walking course with benches placed around the path. There is an older couple sharing a bench with their son, eating kimbap and drinking cans of beer. A middle-aged ajŏssi sits on another bench, wearing shiny white sneakers, smoking a cigarette, and drinking a beer. He is engrossed in a television program that appears on his tiny cell phone screen.

As I walk around the path, I notice a portly halabŏji, at least seventy years old; sitting alone, he innocently gives me a smile and makes strong eye contact with me. As I round the corner, coming closer to him, he says, "The weather's nice today. The air is good here. Sit down next to your oppa for a moment."

I give him a friendly smile. "Yes, the air is nice. It's very quiet, too. Bye now." I bow and walk away. As I continue my slow stroll, something in me feels sad for him and for me. I am curious; maybe his wife has died and he is very lonely. Instead of leaving the walking path, I continue around, like I'm going to take a second lap. I'm ten feet away from him, and I see him pat the concrete bench, beckoning me to sit next to him.

"You came back! Sit down next to your oppa." He smiles. "You're not Korean. Right?" I've tried to evade this question many times before, but people usually keep asking questions until I surrender. Like a recorder, I push the button to play the story I've told at least a thousand times. We inevitably make the usual small talk about my adoption, but now, I am curious about him.

"Are you married?"

"Of course."

"Where is your wife?"

"She's at driving school right now. I've been driving since 1989, but she wanted to learn recently. How old are you? Are you married?"

"No, I'm not married. I am thirty, but I'm not ready to get married yet."

He begins to heavily flirt with me—in a way that makes me just a tad uncomfortable—but I am more amused and find it kind of endearing. "How about going to the convenience store with me. Let's get some beer. Or let's go to Namsan Park or Yeoiudo Park. I can drive us.

Or we can go to your house. You live alone, right? I bet you are lonely. And you're a woman, and I'm a man." He is so much older than I am, and seemingly harmless, so I just smile and laugh.

"No, we are not going anywhere together. We are not going on a date. I am going soon."

"But you can't go. I have a pretty ajumma sitting next to me."

"Why do you call me ajumma? I'm not an ajumma. I'm not married yet. So that makes me an *agassi*, right?" As he keeps inching closer and closer to me, I inch closer to the end of the bench.

"Yes. You are right, agassi. You are Miss. Miss what?"

"Yang. Miss Yang. And you are Mr. what?"

"Kim. Mr. Kim. How about it, Miss Yang? Let's go to your op'isŭt'el."

"Mr. Kim! What are you talking about? We are not a couple, and you are married!"

"Oh . . . yes. I am married . . . that's right."

I have no idea where this conversation is going; I'm not really uncomfortable, but I know it is time to leave. I stand up. "I've got to go. It was very nice meeting you, Mr. Kim."

He looks at me with schoolboyish, longing eyes. "Don't go, Miss Yang."

"Mr. Kim. I have to go." I extend my hand to shake his. He holds on to it for more than a moment.

"Miss Yang. It was very nice to meet you. Don't go so soon." He brings my hand to his mouth and sweetly kisses it. I gently withdraw my hand from his, give him a big smile and a little bow, and slowly walk away.

dash-1 bus

In Buamdong,[17] close to Jahamun Tunnel, there is a bus stop that can be confusing, especially for children. There are two buses with similar routes, but one bus takes the tunnel and another one goes over the tunnel through a residential area, where there are some schools.

A little girl, not older than ten and wearing her summer school uniform, waits at the bus stop, which is about one hundred feet from the tunnel entrance. She motions for the bus to stop, and she climbs on as quickly as she can. She settles into the front seat, right behind the bus driver, as he accelerates toward the tunnel as if a race has just begun.

Suddenly, loud and high, she cries, "Ajŏssi! Why are you going into this tunnel?"

He replies, "This bus takes the tunnel! You need the dash-1 bus."

Upset and almost crying, she says, "Oh my gosh! What do I do?"

bravo your life!

The bus driver lectures her that she should be careful to get on the right bus, and she listens to him as her eyes well up with tears. About thirty feet into the tunnel, I see him look into the rearview mirror, and he slams on the brakes while opening the doors.

"Child, be careful. Next time, don't get on this bus."

She looks scared, but she has no choice but to get off, so she hesitantly says, "Ajŏssi, thank you," and steps down from the bus as quickly as she got on it. I'm surprised by all of this, but no one on the bus seems to think it is wrong or even unsafe. The bus pulls away as fast as it stopped, and as we gain momentum, I turn around to look for the little girl. I see the small silhouette of her body, running along the wall of the tunnel, disappearing into the light.

Ch'ŏnggukchang

Ch'ŏnggukchang is a kind of stinky Korean stew made from fermented soybeans. It is the stronger brother of *toenjang* soup, which is the Korean version of Japanese miso soup. The first time I tried ch'ŏnggukchang, I was so overwhelmed by the strong odor that I could only take a couple of spoonfuls, but for the same reason I love stinky bleu cheese, ch'ŏnggukchang grew on me.

In Samcheongdong[18] there is a restaurant in a traditional Korean home that is famous for its ch'ŏnggukchang. It could possibly be the best ch'ŏnggukchang in Seoul. Its location makes you feel like you are in a special ch'ŏnggukchang club because it is so hard to find. Since I've been a regular customer for the last four years, they know me pretty well. It's a family-run business, but I'm still not exactly sure who is related to whom.

I usually go in by myself. I don't have that many friends, and most foreigners, and even some Koreans, don't like this smelly stew. At first, I think, they felt bad that I was always alone, because Koreans don't eat by themselves, especially on weekend evenings. Now they are used to me, and they are surprised when I occasionally come with someone else.

As I wait for my ch'ŏnggukchang and *banch'an* to arrive, the ajumma I know best kneels down by my table. She wears her hair in a curly bob, has rimless glasses, and has an inquisitive smile. She says, "They told me my favorite English speaker is here."

"Oh . . . thank you. How have you been?" She smiles and says she is great. My food arrives, and she walks back to the next room to dry and sort through the pile of clean chopsticks and spoons.

It's late, almost nine o'clock, and besides a group of ten people in their twenties finishing up their meals, I am alone. I used to never feel weird eating alone, but as time passes in Seoul, sometimes the pitying looks Koreans give me when I'm by myself make me feel like a loser. So, I put on my MP3 player and listen to music to drown out the noise and sorry stares from the group of young Koreans eating, drinking, and having fun.

As the restaurant lights are dimmed, and I'm the only one left, I try to eat faster, scraping the bottom of the cast-iron ch'ŏnggukchang pot with my spoon. The ajumma I know best kneels down next to me one more time. "Wow. You ate all your ch'ŏnggukchang. You must really like it. That's interesting, because most Americans would never eat this."

Another ajumma, who is relatively new to me, says, "Did you say she is American?"

"Yes. She is American. She was born in Korea, but she grew up in America. So, that makes her American. Am I not right?"

"Yes. I see your point. She's American."

Even though I don't consider myself fully American, nor Korean, I am too tired to argue the finer points of cultural and national identity in the Korean language; so I nod my head and smile. The ajumma I know best says, "I think when your mother was pregnant with you she must have eaten a lot of ch'ŏnggukchang, because it's very special the way you like ch'ŏnggukchang so much."

I say, "I'm not sure. I've never thought about it like that."

The other ajumma jumps in, "Yes. That's right. When I was pregnant with my son, I craved a lot of really spicy food. When my son was only two years old, he wanted to eat spicy food all the time. To this day, he loves spicy food."

The ajumma I know best says, "Yes. When I was pregnant, I ate *kalbi* all the time. When my son was a child, and even now, he always says to me, 'Mom, let's eat kalbi!' or 'I want to eat kalbi!'"

Even though I think their theory is a little out there, I am entertained by it. I say, "Next time I see my mother, I will ask her if she ate a lot of ch'ŏnggukchang when she was pregnant."

The ajumma I know best says, "Of course . . . that is what you must do, and tell me her answer next time you are in here."

I stand up, pay my bill, and step down on the ledge to put my shoes on. As I walk into the courtyard I hear the ajumma I know best tell the other ajumma my whole adoption story. I pause for a moment to listen: "She was five kilos when she was born. She was the fifth daughter. Her father was in the hospital, and her family had no money or rice. They had so much hardship. Because she was such a big and healthy baby, her mother thought she was strong enough to go to America—that she would have a better life there . . ."

I smile at the random connection I have with the ajumma I know best, and I walk out the door with my little belly full of ch'ŏnggukchang.

fertility shot

Minam has been trying to have a baby for over four years. Although they have been told there is no reason why they can't conceive, she has turned to frequent trips to the fertility clinic. After lunch at our parents' home, Minam is preparing to take a syringe to a local clinic for her weekly injection. She pulls it out of her purse, and my sisters and mother tell her to save her ten thousand wŏn and do it herself. Ŏmma is a tough, no-frills woman who gave birth to most of her children by herself, out on her balcony. She jumps in, saying, "Minam-ah! Let me inject you. I can do it easily."

"Really? Do you think you can do it?"

"Of course! Come over here." Ŏmma is sitting on the sofa with me. I scoot to the edge; Ŏmma beckons Minam to lie face down in the middle of the sofa.

It's just us women, and Ŏmma pulls down Minam's pants a bit. "Wow! You have a big butt!" Minam feels embarrassed. I laugh, because although what is happening is weird, this kind of scene doesn't surprise me anymore. Our older sisters take a little soju to disinfect the area and smile approvingly.

Ŏmma has bad eyes from her diabetes; she studies the syringe as well as Minam's butt, and then acts quickly. I can tell she has never used a syringe before—she has only received the poke—and she doesn't apply enough pressure. The needle barely lances the skin, and Ŏmma begins to release the fluid prematurely. Our eyes meet with an intense, worried look for a split second, and my other sisters start to yell at her to push it harder. The fluid is running down Minam's large butt cheek, and Ŏmma gives a final good, hard push. About half of the fluid makes it into her system, but we all try to cover for Ŏmma.

Minam complains, "Oh my god. Did it all go in? Why is it wet?"

Ŏmma says, "Don't worry. Ninety-five percent of it went in."

Minam pulls up her cotton stretchy pants. "How much of it went in? That is expensive medicine!"

My older sisters reassure her that almost all of it went in, but we all know the truth. Our mother tries to hide her guilty look. Minam looks at me for an answer, and I quickly glance at Ŏmma. All I can do is remain silent and nod my head.

muji

Muji is my favorite store in Korea, even though it's Japanese. They sell no-name clothing, stationery, and kitchen goods as well as home furnishings. I go there at least twice a week on the way to my health club. Today I notice a man there who looks familiar; I can tell he recognizes me, too. As we stop for a brief moment to stare at each other, it hits me that he is Joanne's brother, Peter Kyungsu. Although I only met him once for about ten minutes, I've seen many of his childhood and more recent photographs. We laugh and point at each other.

Joanne has been back in New York for a while, and because I miss her so much, I'm delighted to see him. Peter Kyungsu is a couple of years older than Joanne and I, and he recently started working for one of Samsung's design departments. He is smart and witty, with a complexion that is as flawless as a baby's bum. I've become quite scared of his sarcasm and his opinions, because Joanne has told me how critical he can be of other people's fashion sense and style.

Joanne always said Peter and I would meet here one day, because we both have the same Muji floor chairs that are like minimalist recliners but without arms or legs. We begin to talk, and I'm curious about his new job and how his sister is doing. Since our legs are tired of standing, we sit down on two Muji display chairs. All the store employees know us and insa as they walk by, but I don't think they knew that we know each other. We talk for about fifteen minutes. As we part, I compliment him on his expensive, spotless sneakers, and he mentions my new MP3 player. A day later, I send him an email about my job at Korea University, because his friend in the States is interested in finding a teaching position in Seoul. He responds—thanking me for the information—and adding:

> *It was good to see you and your holographic-pattern coat. You reminded me of the Long Island girls that get all dolled up to hang out at the local shopping mall on the weekend. Oh well. Nice iPod shuffle. I have to go back to Muji tomorrow to get some travel accessories. I'm off to Milan for a week on Monday.*

I feel weird and a little embarrassed about his words, and later that night, I tell John Lee about his email. He laughs loudly, "That shit is funny!" Now I'm officially scared of Joanne's brother. I wasn't even dressed up when I met him: I had come from work.

A few days later I'm back at Muji again, wearing a strange outfit that I regretted the second I stepped on the bus, but it's too late to go home and change. Out of the corner of my eye, while looking at the skirts and pants on the rack, I see Peter Kyungsu leisurely stroll into the men's section; I freak out, nearly dropping the item I'm holding. I immediately run out of our favorite store as fast as I can— praying he doesn't see me.

massage ajumma

I now live on the second floor of an old house in Seoul. The owners, a traditional Korean couple, live below Peter and me. Even though we aren't related, every month when we pay the rent we call them Halmŏni and Halabŏji, Grandmother and Grandfather.

Halmŏni had a stroke a couple of years ago, and it left her partially paralyzed. It impaired her speech, and she walks with her left leg slightly dragging behind her. On Thursdays, an ajumma comes to their home and gives her an hour-long massage.

As I walk into our shared entryway, their first-floor door is wide open. There, in the main room of their home, Halmŏni lies on her side while the massage ajumma confidently pounds and rubs her in sort of a circular motion. The massage ajumma looks to be in her early sixties, maybe ten years younger than Halmŏni. I can't help but stand and stare, imagining how nice and relaxing that massage must be.

After a brief moment, they notice me. The massage ajumma says, "I used to be like her. I had a stroke and my body was partially paralyzed, and after I had regular massages, my body is completely better."

Impressed by all of this, I hesitantly ask, "If you have time, could you come upstairs and give me a massage? I didn't have a stroke, but I've been very stressed lately." She says that she can come up in an hour; Halmŏni nods her head approvingly.

Waiting upstairs, I watch Korean TV and eat my ramen, and even though an hour hasn't passed, I hear a knock on the door. As I open the door, the massage ajumma is hot and panting from the heat, and she's delighted to feel my air conditioning. I explain that I need to finish my ramen quickly; she tells me to take my time. She curiously walks around the main room, and just as I shovel a large amount of noodles into my mouth, she begins to take off her t-shirt and baggy cotton shorts. I'm so surprised that I semi-choke on the noodles, startling her. She tries to cover her body with her hands. "Oh my gosh! Is there a man in the apartment?" she asks.

Staring at her buxom body and sagging breasts held up with a very big bra, I clear my throat. "Oh no. My boyfriend's not here. Don't worry. Make yourself comfortable." She looks relieved and tells me that she's just too hot and that it's more comfortable with her clothes off—she can't take them off downstairs, because the halabŏji is always there.

I tell her to come in and watch TV, giving her the remote control. While I finish my noodles and polish off the kimch'i, she sits on the floor in her bra and panties, flipping through the channels, settling on a program about children and puppies.

After I'm finished, she tells me to lie on the floor next to her. Any vision I had of a professional masseuse in my home helping me to relieve stress instantly dissipates as she begins the massage with the TV on at high volume. Her breasts keep brushing and bouncing up against my body. She finds the program so adorable that there isn't any way I can ask her to turn it down or off. But her hands are magic, and as my body becomes putty, I tune out the TV. I am only aware that it is on when she gives a low laugh or says, "Too bad you can't see this. You would love it."

She rubs and pounds in a circular motion with the kind of specialized knowledge that can only come from years of experience. I am eased into a state between sleep and consciousness. Finally, she pushes my body up, so I sit staring directly at the TV. She pats my shoulders three times and says, "I'm finished. The program is finished. Good timing. You missed a great show."

I am so relaxed that all I can bring myself to say is, "That was amazing. Can you come next Thursday?"

"Of course. I can come every week," she says, putting her t-shirt and shorts back on. I pay her twenty thousand wŏn, and she smiles. I open the door, and the humid heat meets her once again.

shower rescue

I have just put shampoo in my hair when the petite and cheerful locker-room ajumma with permed, frizzy hair, a strong overbite, and bright red lipstick comes into the health club shower room. She has an announcement: "Ladies. Excuse me ladies. A repairman will be here in five minutes. You must exit the shower room in five minutes. Please cover up the moment you get to your locker. You can return shortly after."

There is a mass exodus of middle-aged ajummas who had been hanging out in the sauna. I lather my hair as quickly as I can and then throw in the conditioner. Pleased with how fast I do this, I think I have two minutes to soak in the green-tea hot tub—my legs are sore from my workout. In what seems like thirty seconds, everyone is gone except me, and a huge, thick plastic curtain is strung across the double-door entrance to the locker room.

The red lipstick ajumma bursts through the door to find only me in the green-tea tub. Our eyes meet with an intensity that is both worrisome and playful. "Oh my god! You're still in here! He's in the locker room! What do we do?"

"I'm sorry. I thought I had five minutes. I went as fast as I could, but then I saw the plastic curtain and didn't know what to do."

"Wait here a moment." She leaves and then shortly returns with a dark orange, thick woolen blanket. I stand next to her—shivering and naked—and she's in her work uniform, although I've seen her naked many times. She wraps the blanket around me tightly. "Are you ready?"

I nod my head and she opens the double doors, sweeping the heavy plastic curtain aside. With the blanket draped around my entire body, and her arms wrapped tightly around me, we emerge from the dark shower room into the bright locker room; I feel like a survivor being rescued from a burning home. The other ajummas, many of whom I've come to know through the years, start clapping and whistling at me. My sauna ajumma yells out, "Oooh! It's our sexy Mi Soon who was still in there!" as she stands next to the repairman, who tries to avoid eye contact with me.

As the repairman marches into the shower room, the red lipstick ajumma walks me to my locker and gives me a little back rub while hugging me. She laughs and tells me how lucky I am that she checked one last time. After a couple of minutes, another ajumma announces that the repairman will exit the shower room. The second after he leaves, the locker room returns to normal, buzzing with the sounds of hair dryers, makeup application, and a lot of gossip. The red lipstick ajumma removes my blanket and smiles. "You can go back in now."

"she's adopted . . ."

I'm taking care of two amazing children this weekend. Their white American mother, Sharon, is in Rome for an energy conference. She was a Peace Corps volunteer in Korea twenty-seven years ago, and she never really left Seoul after she arrived. Sharon married a Korean man some years back, but now they are divorced and she is raising their children alone. Korea remains a surprisingly xenophobic society, but her children, who speak Korean as a first language and are fluent in English as well, are two of the most amazing and well-adjusted kids I've ever met. Jiyoung is an outgoing ten-year-old girl with a sensitive spirit, and shy Sangho is a quiet and clever nine-year-old boy.

 I'm with them for the weekend, and we are visiting the Seodaemun Prison Museum, where Korean nationals were imprisoned, tortured, or killed during the Japanese occupation from 1910–1945. Sangho is extremely curious about the museum, and he takes in every bit of the grounds, making sure we don't miss one building. Since it's Saturday, the place is filled with Korean kids on field trips with their hagwŏns.

When you see these beautiful children, it is clear that they are not "pure blooded" Koreans. And even though I am old enough to be their mother, I can relate to them, especially when I recall my own childhood memories. All three of us have lived in the comfortable middle class, but the majority of people in the mainstream see us as outsiders with a native language that doesn't match our faces.

As we are looking at the prison cells, some of the other children nearby hear Sangho's perfect Korean, but the moment they see his face, they yell out to each other, "Hey, everyone, look at the foreigner!" I know he hears what they say, but he ignores them. I notice how everyone looks at him and his sister with curiosity, especially when they speak. I know how this feels, as a young woman speaking Korean with a foreign accent in Seoul.

The same way that I am honest to all Koreans about being a Korean adoptee, I have told Jiyoung and Sangho all about my two families in Seoul and Minnesota. When we rode in the taxi to the museum, Sangho immediately told the driver that I am adopted and don't speak Korean well. He does it again at the Chinese restaurant, where we eat black bean noodles for lunch, and in the taxi during the ride home. Now, we walk into their neighborhood grocery store, and the ajumma working there greets them energetically; Sangho tells her as quickly as he can that I am adopted. Lastly, walking up to their home, we run into a Korean family living a few doors down from them. The mother is very kind and asks affectionately how they are doing; the father stands to the side smiling while their son and daughter talk to Jiyoung. I know what is coming next, and I smile at Sangho, encouraging him to tell my story as dramatically as he wants to. He proceeds. "Did you know my babysitter was adopted? She went to America when she was a baby. And she knows her Korean family, too. That is why her Korean sounds so strange . . ."

batman

It's our aunt's sixtieth birthday; she is Ŏmma's younger sister. A sixtieth birthday is a milestone in Korean culture. Miok came up from Daegu for the occasion, and for the first time in a couple of years, all five sisters are together. It feels exciting and comfortable. Finally, my Korean is good enough that I can fluently converse with them.

We met in Namdaemun, where Minam and K'ŭn Ŏnni work. After thirty minutes of coordinating our locations, we are now waiting for the bus. It's rush hour, and if you've never experienced Seoul's public transportation at this time, it can best be described as after-Christmas shopping sales in America on crack cocaine—times ten.

Our bus arrives, and the five of us push onto it so we can be together. Because I didn't grow up with our Korean family, I'm often amused and fascinated when I see all of my sisters in action. I wonder if this is how I would have turned out. They are loud, funny, bickering at the top of their lungs, overly talkative to strangers, and very intense. Everyone on the crowded bus stares at them, like they are putting on a show, but there is absolutely no affectation; they are just completely absorbed in our Yang family world.

Minam is tired, and she grabs a coveted seat. The rest of us pile our bags onto her lap and around her feet. The seat in front of Minam opens up, and Chagŭn Ŏnni sits with relief; Miok sits on her lap. Just as the bags are redistributed between the two seats, a halmŏni boards the bus with a baby secured to her back in the traditional Korean way. Miok and Chagŭn Ŏnni take a deep breath, laugh, and stand up, beckoning the halmŏni to the newly open seat. The baby is really tiny, and there is a satin gold cape tied around the halmŏni's neck, completely covering the quiet but fidgeting baby. Miok and Chagŭn Ŏnni stand right next to the grandmother, holding on to her seat tightly.

Chagŭn Ŏnni touches the gold, satin cape and says, "Halmŏni, what are you, Batman? Why are you wearing this Batman cape?"

Miok starts to touch the head of the baby, "*Ŏmŏ! Ŏmŏ!* What is this? A puppy?"

Everyone is staring, and I can't help but laugh; I touch the baby's head, too, wondering if it is a little puppy on the halmŏni's back. Miok lifts up the cape and a tiny, cute baby—not more than three months old—appears, wearing a puffy cotton hat.

Miok says, "Oh! So cute! Halmŏni, I think your baby is too hot with the cape on." She feels the baby's cheeks. "You should take the hat off, too." And without the halmŏni's consent, she moves the cape to the side and removes the hat. Chagŭn Ŏnni and the halmŏni get into a deep conversation, while Miok and I touch the baby's cheeks and talk about how cute she is. Minam and K'ŭn Ŏnni look at the baby, too; Minam is envious, as she has been trying to get pregnant for years now.

She looks at me and whispers, "Mi Soon-ah, that baby is not cute!" She says even more quietly, "*Hobak!* That baby has a huge pumpkin face!"

K'ŭn Ŏnni and I hit her for being so mean and shallow, but it's sadly true that almost all Koreans are obsessed with physical appearance—even babies cannot escape this fact.

The next bus stop is the halmŏni's, and she asks Miok to put the hat back on and secure the cape over the baby. As the halmŏni exits the bus, Chagŭn Ŏnni yells, "Goodbye, Batman! Batman, Goodbye!"

so shim

So Shim is a vegetarian restaurant in Insadong specializing in all-natural Korean food. Their simple menu uses ingredients that come from mountain vegetation, and some of the side dishes can be found in Buddhist temple cuisine. Through the years I have enjoyed countless meals there. The bubbly owner is extremely kind and always inquires about what is going on in my life. Yoo Jin, the long-term ajumma cook, always gives me a couple of extra side dishes that don't go with the standard bibimbap meal. The three of us enjoy each other's company so much that we often get lost in conversation, and it seems like we are good friends, even though both of them are old enough to be my mother.

When Peter first came to Seoul, I took him to So Shim for his inaugural Korean meal; he fell in love with their food immediately, and this became one of our favorite places to dine. Because Peter is so charming, handsome, and genuinely kind, everyone we meet in Korea adores him. The So Shim ladies are extra enthusiastic about him. Every time we have come in, they have doted on us and told us what an attractive and well-matched couple we are.

As the months have gone by, Peter and I have become busy with work and our lives, and we have had less and less time to visit So Shim together. The last few times I was there alone, I successfully tiptoed around their questions about Peter.

Today, the owner chirps, "Yoo Jin-ah! Yoo Jin-ah! Miss Yang is here!"

Both of them give me big smiles and hugs. I sit down at my favorite table, closest to the kitchen and counter; they immediately bring me traditional barley water and take my order.

Yoo Jin says, "Miss Yang. Where is Peter? Why don't you come with Peter anymore?"

It is quiet and no one is around, so I reply, "I'm sorry to tell you this, but Peter and I broke up."

There is dead silence. Their faces become ghostly white, and their smiles drop off instantly. In unison, they ask, "But why? I don't understand. You're the perfect couple."

"I don't understand either. It is very complicated. And it is even harder for me to explain in Korean." Yoo Jin begins to cry, not dramatically, but tears roll down her face; she cannot find anything more to say. The owner manages to ask a few more questions that I am unable to answer. An awkward silence takes over, and a few minutes later, Yoo Jin brings my bowl of bibimbap, giving me even more side dishes than usual. I eat the meal quickly; they look at me sadly. Finally, after I pay, I tell them, "I'm sorry I can't explain more, but Peter and I are still best friends. There is even a chance we could get back together . . ."

Smiles instantly return to their faces. I walk out the door, wondering if this will really happen.

treadmill

As I walk on a treadmill at the health club, I flip through the eighty or so channels on my personal TV. It's a great way to pass time. It's mostly Korean TV, with a few English movie channels, and I usually watch dramas to help my listening skills, especially since I have very little time to study Korean these days. Nothing is catching my eye, so I settle on the cheesy program about Korean adoptees who are reunited with their birth mothers, either abroad or on Korean soil. Many adoptees were sent out of Korea after the war, especially in the seventies and eighties; some went to the States, while others were sent to Western European countries.

This program is an exploitative work of art, using every possible ploy to tug at the heartstrings of the prime-time Korean viewers—mostly ajummas, I think. It sets everything up so dramatically, from the tearful story of the birth mother to the curiosity, masked by indifference, of the adopted child who finally breaks down in tears. If that isn't enough, the main host, a nerdy Korean actor with a strong overbite, is always alongside a beautiful Korean *t'aellŏnt'u* or singer who gladly takes the opportunity to show her Korean fans her sensitive and caring side.

Today they are in the French countryside, and the young woman who will be reunited with her birth mother is a doctor who's married to a white French guy; they have a baby as well. The adoptee was placed when she was twelve years old, very late in life, but she seems to have lost all her Korean. It must have been hard for her to lose her family and culture at that age—to have to rebuild and become French.

In the show, she watches a translated video message from her Korean mother, and her tears come for the first time. The music becomes more dramatic, and Korean words appear on the screen: *30 minutes before they meet.* As this continues, the words move from minutes to meters. The mother arrives in an SUV, and she gets out alone and stands there for a while crying (most likely because she was told to wait there so she could be filmed), while the daughter stands with the Korean t'aellŏnt'u and program host. They are maybe one hundred yards apart, and in case you can't tell, the TV screen flashes the distance in Korean, until they are only ten meters apart and still counting.

The music is working its magic, and it's starting to get to me. As the mother and daughter come closer, they run to each other and hug and cry. The mother's face is red from her tears, and her Korean words are laced with grief and guilt. In a strange way, I feel relieved that I can understand everything she says to her daughter, because when I first met my birth family I couldn't understand one word of Korean. The daughter doesn't understand anything her birth mother says. I'm mad at myself for being touched by this show, yet my heart sinks even more when the birth mother dries her daughter's tears and lovingly says, "Your life was so hard, you forgot all your Korean, didn't you?"

The daughter answers *yes* in French.

I look to both sides and notice an ajumma and a younger woman watching the same show as they walk on their treadmills. All three of us wipe some tears from our eyes—all for the same reason: Because this part of the show is honestly sad.

two towels

I'm tired of being told that I should get married soon; I have stayed away from my birth family for over a month to avoid the when-are-you-going-to-get-married questions. I begin to sympathize with any Korean woman who is in my predicament but has no American family to turn to for affirmation of her single, free life. Ŏmma still doesn't understand my life these days: Before, I was working at a good university in Seoul, and she wanted me to marry Peter. Now I am single and writing full time.

In spite of this, I decide to spend the weekend at my parents' house. About a day into my stay, I realize the merits of an afternoon-only visit. Ŏmma has a regular routine that revolves around everyone else's needs except hers, and my long weekend stay is throwing her off. Plus, their bedtime and morning wake-up time are strange for me.

On Saturday at 4:30 a.m., the fluorescent lights are abruptly turned on, and Ŏmma is cooking a full Korean breakfast for my father before he goes to work. When I sleep at their home, comfortable Korean bedding is placed on the floor of the main room, right next to the two refrigerators, two freezers, and a water dispenser, which sits on top of a cabinet that holds standard Korean shower towels—the size of American hand towels. (Anytime one of the massive refrigerators or freezers is opened, I smile with satisfaction, because it's filled to the brim with all kinds of Korean food. My birth family suffered from serious food shortages in the not-so-distant past.)

It is loud, as usual, and I smell pungent kimch'i stew boiling on the stove. I reach for my earplugs, which came out in the middle of the night, and I grab a towel out of the cabinet to cover my eyes from the bright lights. I fall back asleep.

I wake up around 10:00 a.m. Ŏmma is in a crabby mood, and she brusquely tells me to take a shower and then she'll make me breakfast. Taking two hand towels into the bathroom, I use one to wrap around my hair and the other to dry my body. As I walk out, she is cleaning, and I hand her the two towels; she gives me a strange look. I can tell she wants to say something. "Mi Soon. Why do you use so many towels? You don't need two towels!"

I feel surprised and try to explain, but she continues to complain about my towel usage in an even louder voice. "I'm not going to wash these two towels. You can reuse them tomorrow. And don't use two towels next time."

I feel quite frustrated and think she is being irrational, and because I'm not a morning person, I'm extra annoyed. "Ŏmma, wash them. Because I'm never going to sleep here again. Now you don't have to worry about me using two towels, ever!"

I tell her that I'm going to leave now. She is quite surprised by my words, but she acts defensive and tough. "But what about your breakfast?"

"I don't need any. I can get something when I leave."

"No. Let me make you breakfast. What are you going to eat?"

"I'm fine. I don't need breakfast. I will get something near the subway."

At this point we are both acting overly dramatic; I pack my bag, and she throws the two towels into the washing machine. She slams the door loudly. Just as I'm about to walk out the door, she says, "Mi Soon. You can sleep here another night."

But my feelings are hurt because of how fast her moods change with me—I think she should be happy for the time we spend together. Miok always tries to reassure me that she is this way with everyone, that everyone "fights well with Ŏmma."

Ŏmma starts to act overly kind to me again, but I can't change back as fast as she does. "Ŏmma. I know it is hard for you to have me here sometimes, because there isn't a lot of space. So, I am sorry. I will visit you again, but I won't sleep here anymore."

She is surprised by my honesty, and as I walk down the stairs, she yells out, "Mi Soon-ah! Sleep here again . . . You can use two towels!"

scooter lesbians

I pull up in front of Tous Les Jour bakery, and Joanne is waiting there listening to her iPod. She doesn't know it is me in front of her with my helmet, white mask, and sunglasses. It takes her a few seconds to realize it's me, and then she bursts out laughing. "I thought you were one of those weird ajŏssi!"

Within seconds, she's on the back of my scooter and we're tearing down the small alleyways of Seoul. I take her for a ttŏkbokki dinner, and it's like we are on one of our famous friendship dates again. We sing songs and scream like children, happy to experience familiar Seoul in a new way.

Women don't ride scooters here. In some countryside areas, women who ride scooters are prostitutes, but in Seoul, scooters and motorcycles are reserved mostly for men holding large tin containers of Chinese or Korean food, delivery men with huge A-frames attached to the backs of their bikes, and a few hipster guys with their sexy girlfriends hugging them from behind. My scooter is a Hyosung Romance Cruise, and it's only 49 cc, but we act like we are on a Harley-Davidson.

We are going from Insadong to Chungmuro[19] for another helmet. We're at the corner of Gyeongbuk Palace, and the crosswalk light is taking forever. We are in our own world, and I'm singing at the top of my lungs, *You got to know when to hold 'em, know when to fold 'em—know when to walk away, and know when to run—you never count your money, when you're sittin' at the table—they'll be time enough for countin', when the dealin's done . . .*

I look to my left. A man in his thirties is staring at us, and it's obvious he wants to say something. The light still hasn't changed, and he finally says, in perfect English, "Excuse me. By chance, are you two lesbians?"

Joanne starts laughing uncontrollably, and I do as well. "No. We're not. We're best friends, though."

"Oh, I'm sorry. I was hoping you were lesbians, because I'm a reporter for the *Seoul Times*, and I'm writing a story about lesbians in Seoul, but no one will let me interview them because of their families. I just thought you were lesbians because I've never seen two girls on a scooter before."

The light turns green. Joanne says, "Sorry, sir. Gotta go. Good luck with your story." We zoom off into the evening, taking the crosswalk as if we are pedestrians—because when you have a scooter in Seoul, you can go anywhere.

present

I walk into one of my favorite boutiques in Myeongdong. The petite and friendly fashion designer and shop owner is not there. She has a few stores around Seoul, but the Myeongdong location is her flagship store. She makes creative clothes using pure cotton or wool, and the textiles are all designed and made in Korea. I try on a new black dress that can double as a short-sleeve trench coat, and I think it is quite cute. As I make my purchase, the owner walks in; she is happy to see me because I was in America for most of the summer. She walks up to me with a big smile. "Oh my god! You've lost so much weight. You look great!"

"Oh. Um, yes I lost some weight because I was in the hospital for a week at the beginning of the summer."

"I see. Well, you look great. You were really a little fat the first time I met you." I blush from embarrassment; other customers are eavesdropping. I'm about to walk out the door, but she stops me for a moment. She walks to a shelf and takes down a small, gray, long-sleeve cotton shirt beneath an even smaller, sleeveless, green wool shirt that has a pattern of high-heeled shoes on it. She hands it to me. "Present. Here is a present for you because you've lost so much weight. You can wear them together or separately."

I blush even more. I say thank you, put it in my bag, give her insa, and walk out the door. I'm touched by her kindness, but I feel a little uneasy about why I received this present.

laundry basket lettuce

Ŏmma has a special kind of garden every spring and summer, one that she is very proud of. In front of their humble home, positioned close to the heavy black gate, are five large, dark green laundry baskets filled to the top with rich, black soil. They are in the tiny alleyway. Even though there isn't one tiny patch of grass at their home, Ŏmma manages to make a vegetable and flower garden every year—in makeshift pots and baskets—growing anything from tomatoes, lettuce, and hot peppers to beautiful geraniums and marigolds. The batches of small lettuce heads came up beautifully this summer—lime green in color, as soft as rice paper—and are ready for us to eat. Since a lack of food took me away from my Korean family and sent me to my American family, I think Ŏmma experiences a sense of fulfillment now when she feeds me.

K'ŭn Ŏnni mixes soy sauce, spicy red pepper paste, sesame oil, sugar, and sesame seeds into a sweet-and-spicy sauce. She sets this on the table along with various other banch'an, steaming bowls of rice, and toenjang soup. Grabbing the delicate lettuce greens, we each hold a bunch in our left palm, scoop a bit of rice and sauce into them, fold them together, and then stuff them into our mouths simultaneously. We are eating quickly, even aggressively, and the greens that had filled the large aluminum bowl quickly become depleted. Ŏmma notices this, along with how much I am loving her homegrown lettuce, and like a powerful ajumma at E-mart[20] snapping up the last hot sale item, she grabs the metal bowl and shoves it under the table, announcing loudly, "This last lettuce is for Mi Soon!"

After a few more bites of banch'an I take the remaining greens, use my spoon to dish some rice and sauce into them, shove the big bunch in my mouth, and chew well, happily looking at my mother. She gives me a satisfied smile.

yogurt

I don't see K'ŭn Ŏnni that often, especially lately, because she has a new job. She is a Yakult[21] ajumma, one of the many ladies in Korea who wear matching yellow jackets and hats and push yellow, refrigerated motorized carts filled with all kinds of yogurt. They deliver daily orders to the various businesses, shop owners, schools, and homes of people who live in each tongne. My sister has a route near her house. She works six days a week, but Sundays are hers; she usually stays at home watching TV, eating, and sleeping all day because her legs are so tired.

When she sees me, she hugs me the way a mother hugs her child, lovingly tight, lingering in a few extra seconds of closeness. There are seventeen years between us, so she well remembers my mother being pregnant with me and then returning home from the hospital empty-handed. I think she and my mother shared a kindred feeling of loss for me, and for this reason, I think of her as my younger mother here in Korea.

Sometimes we go to the mogyok t'ang together. After my first introduction to this place five years ago, with my sisters, nieces, and mother washing my hair and body like I was a little baby, I'm now extremely comfortable being naked, bathing, soaking, and sweating with my family for hours on end. K'ŭn Ŏnni still likes to wash my hair and scrub my back. I let her because I think it helps us make up for lost time. This is the first time we have gone to the mogyok t'ang since she started her new job. Her eyes are tired, and her walk says she is utterly exhausted, but she smiles and talks to me with much passion.

We shampoo our hair and then scrub ourselves with a long piece of slightly abrasive material, which cleanses our bodies and leaves them with frothy white foam everywhere. After we rinse off, we head into the warm green-tea bath, which can fit about ten people. We go in and out of hot water, cold water, a dry sauna, a steam room, and more warm water, repeating this circuit until our skin is prepared for the full body scrub, where we use little exfoliating green mitts on both of our hands. We start with our arms, working in slow, steady movements, and then we do our backs. Little brown bits of skin peel off with ease, and a slight redness appears. The usual next step is a moisturizer, but K'ŭn Ŏnni takes a break and pulls out some Yakult strawberry yogurt from her toiletry bag. She opens it, and just as I think she is going to hand it to me for a little snack, she starts to aggressively pour it over my entire body, rubbing it in vigorously. "Mi Soon-ah, this is very good for your body. It's great moisture."

All I can say is, "Oh. Wow. K'ŭn Ŏnni, this is the first time I've used yogurt like this." It's not over yet. Next comes the small milk carton, and before I can say another word, she dramatically pours it over the yogurt and gives me a full-body, stand-up massage. She's about to open one more container of yogurt, but I stop her. "Save some for yourself!"

She continues to massage me everywhere, and in the midst of her work, she says, "Just one more thing. Don't worry. I've got to do one more thing." She whips out a small bottle of sesame cooking oil and layers it on the rest. I think this is the first time I've ever smelled this combination in my life. After a deep back-and-neck massage, she pours the remaining milk, yogurt, and sesame oil over her body and rubs it in as quickly as possible. We rinse off, towel-dry ourselves, and walk out to the locker room area, where she runs her slightly callous hands along my smooth back and arms, smiles at me, and lovingly says, "Mi Soon-ah, now you are so soft, like my baby."

cheong min

There are five ajummas sitting in a perfect row in the center section of the airplane, closest to the dividing wall and large mounted television. Each lady has a Korean baby on her lap. I walk past them and sit down about ten seats behind them. The moment the plane takes off, all five babies begin to wail. I'm tired, so I put my orange earplugs in and try to nod off.

After the seatbelt sign has been turned off, three of the babies are still crying and need to be walked around the airplane. Although I'd like to sleep, I stand up and walk over to one of the ajummas at the back of the plane; she is bouncing a little baby boy around so he doesn't cry. I walk right up to her, smiling and speaking in Korean, "Hello, my name is Yang Mi Soon. I'm curious. Are these babies being adopted to America?"

"Yes, they are."

"I thought so. I was adopted when I was three months old, and now I live in Seoul. I met my birth family five years ago, and I can speak some Korean. If you need to take a break, I can hold some of the babies."

"Wow. That would be great. Would you mind holding him right now? I need to use the bathroom."

"What's his name?"

"I'm not sure. Jung Min, Sung Min . . . Something with a Min. Look at his wrist."

The ajumma gently places the almost-crying baby boy in my arms. I look closely at the plastic laminated band that is tightly wrapped around his tiny left wrist. The band lists his birthday, in January, his Korean name, Kim Cheong Min, and his new American name, Anthony Leonard. His face is precious, his thick black hair is soft and sticks straight up, his skin is silky soft, and his eyes make me melt. He starts to whimper, just a little, so I begin to rock him back and forth. His eyes meet my gaze, and he begins to smile. I speak in Korean to him because he's ten months old and is used to hearing Korean by now. "Cheong Min-ah, you're so cute. Cheong Min-ah, you're so good. Do you like flying, Cheong Min-ah?" I don't know why, but I can't bring myself to use his English name. I don't want to speak English to him, either.

The ajumma returns from the bathroom; she puts her arms out for Cheong Min, but I tell her that I'd like to hold him a bit longer, if she doesn't mind. She smiles and helps me put him into the front carrier, then she latches the straps snuggly around my back. He's a little heavy, so I feel relieved. I walk him around a little more, kissing his soft head of hair, and then we return to my seat. He's sleeping now.

When I first started living in Seoul, many Korean names seemed strange to me, though my American parents always used my Korean name, because, I guess, Mi Soon is gentle enough on the Western ear. Now, Korean names have meaning to me, and they sound poetic and beautiful.

I hold Cheong Min close to me, kissing his cheeks and forehead, whispering in his ear, putting his name in front of everything I say—"Cheong Min-ah, do you like flying? Cheong Min-ah, are you okay? Cheong Min-ah, you're such a good boy"—because as we fly through each time zone, closer and closer to Kansas, his final destination, I know he may never hear his name like this again.

afterword

I first went to Korea in June of 2001 for a three-week visit on my own. I didn't want to take a motherland tour, but at the same time, I wasn't prepared for everything that Seoul had become: a bustling cosmopolitan city in a hurry, unforgiving to anyone who doesn't speak Korean or move as fast as the locals do.

Within one day of my arrival, the Korean mother of a friend of mine found my birth family by calling the police station and asking for the phone numbers of all couples with the husband's last name, Yang, and wife's last name, Kim, who were old enough to have a twenty-four-year-old daughter. In two phone calls, she located the Yang family. Four older sisters and a younger brother lived in southern Seoul, and only Yang Mi Soon was missing from the family. I was introduced to them immediately. I learned that my name was given to me by my Korean father the day I was born, and that my birthday is truly July 5, 1977—not give or take a few days or months, as my American parents were told when they received me. I began to take pride in my Korean first name, because it is my one piece of identity continuity, having been part of my life since the day I was born.

After returning to America for a year and earning a Fulbright fellowship to move to Korea in the summer of 2002, I began to study Korean, a very slow and laborious process for me as an adult. I moved to Seoul in July of that year, and I stayed for five years. The beginning years were the hardest, but as I learned Korean and slowly broke away the American mold that encapsulated me, even blinded me to the beauty of the "ugly" things in Seoul, a whole new world opened for me: I became especially close to my sisters, made true connections with Korean people (friends as well as people who happened to work where I often went), spoke Korean every day, and became more confident of the layout of Seoul than of some of my favorite American cities.

Through Fulbright, teaching at Korea University, and working as a freelance writer, Seoul became a second home to me. My Korean family graciously accepted that the way I live—and how I interpret the world differently from them—is because of my American upbringing. My Minnesotan family gave me the strong base from which I became the young woman my Korean family is so proud of. I love both of my families and feel close to them in similar yet different ways. And dear friends—Joanne H. Kim, John Lee, and Peter McAuley—helped me navigate Seoul's landscape with ease, making urban living adventurous and fulfilling during my stay in Korea.

Bravo Your Life! has been in the making for a while now. The book began with journal entries, and within a couple of years, the vignette form came to fit all the things I saw and experienced every day. As I moved around this massive city, working and playing, I began to vacillate between—and even get lost—observing contemporary Korean life as an undercover foreigner and living like a native Korean. It is from this vantage point that all my vignettes were born. All the stories are true and date back to the first time I went to

bravo your life!

Seoul in 2001. My one hope for this book is that it opens a window to contemporary Korean society in a fun and funny way.

endnotes

1. Main river in Seoul that divides the city into the North, Gangbuk, and South, Gangnam.
2. Large city in the southeast region of Korea. My immediate family lives in Seoul, except Miok, husband, and children.
3. "Please give me kimbap. Please remove the ham."
4. "We don't have hamburgers."
5. Financial and central area of Seoul where many young people spend time and shop.
6. Plain residential area near Korea University filled with many op'isŭt'els and fried chicken shops.
7. Traditional area of Seoul with many teashops, galleries, and antiques.
8. City in the southern part of the country famous for its bibimbap. Restaurants there use extra ingredients, giving it a different taste.
9. Abbreviation for Korea University, one of the top three universities in Korea.
10. Literally means "university area," but is also an artistic, fun area of Seoul.
11. East gate landmark and huge late-night shopping area of Seoul.
12. Area in northern Seoul, near Myeongdong.
13. Hongik University, a major art area and the most bohemian area of Seoul.
14. Large street in an area of northern Seoul. It runs from Dongdaemun to Insadong.
15. Beautiful Korean dog breed that looks like a husky. Commonly used in dog meat stew.

16 Restored stream in the northern part of Seoul. It's considered an engineering feat, because a huge highway overpass was once located there.
17 Nice, quiet neighborhood near the Korean president's residence.
18 Charming neighborhood north of Insadong, full of traditional places and lovely cafes.
19 Area of Seoul with many motorcycle and pet shops.
20 Like Wal-Mart.
21 Large Japanese yogurt company that has a big presence in Korea.

acknowledgments

Thank you to my American and Korean families, especially my mother, Julie Burzlaff, and my late grandmother, Sylvia Boettger. Additional thanks to Brian Boyd, Hangtae Cho, June Cho, Ellen Hawley, Hyelim Hwang, Joanne H. Kim, John Lee, Vicky Lettmann, and Peter McAuley.

about the author

Mi Soon Burzlaff lives in New York, where she and Joanne Kim are starting an organic kimch'i company. She still visits Seoul regularly.